STEEP
WILD

by **Rodney Legg**,
the island's Warden since 1974,
utilising the research of
naturalist **Tony Parsons**,
photographs by **Colin Graham**,
and the woodcuts of
Thomas Bewick

Wincanton Press
National School, North Street, Wincanton, Somerset BA9 9AT

Publishing details. First published 1990. Copyright © 1990

Provisional permission for copying. This is intended as a source book for information on Steep Holm and material may be quoted from it, providing the source is acknowledged and mention is made of the work of the Kenneth Allsop Memorial Trust in conserving the island. All other rights are reserved.

Printing credits. Typesetting input by Reg Ward at Holwell, Dorset, and output by Wordstream Limited, Poole.
Printed in Somerset by Wincanton Litho at Wessex Way, Wincanton Business Park, Wincanton.

Distribution. By Dorset Publishing Company from the Wincanton Press, National School, North Street, Wincanton, Somerset BA9 9AT. Telephone 0963 32583.
International Standard Book Number. ISBN 0 948699 11 6

To **Timothy Eden**,
the Warden's young inquisitor:
for him to present to **Heinz Sielman**,
the international patriarch of wildlife television,
on the occasion of his visit from Hamburg to Steep Holm.

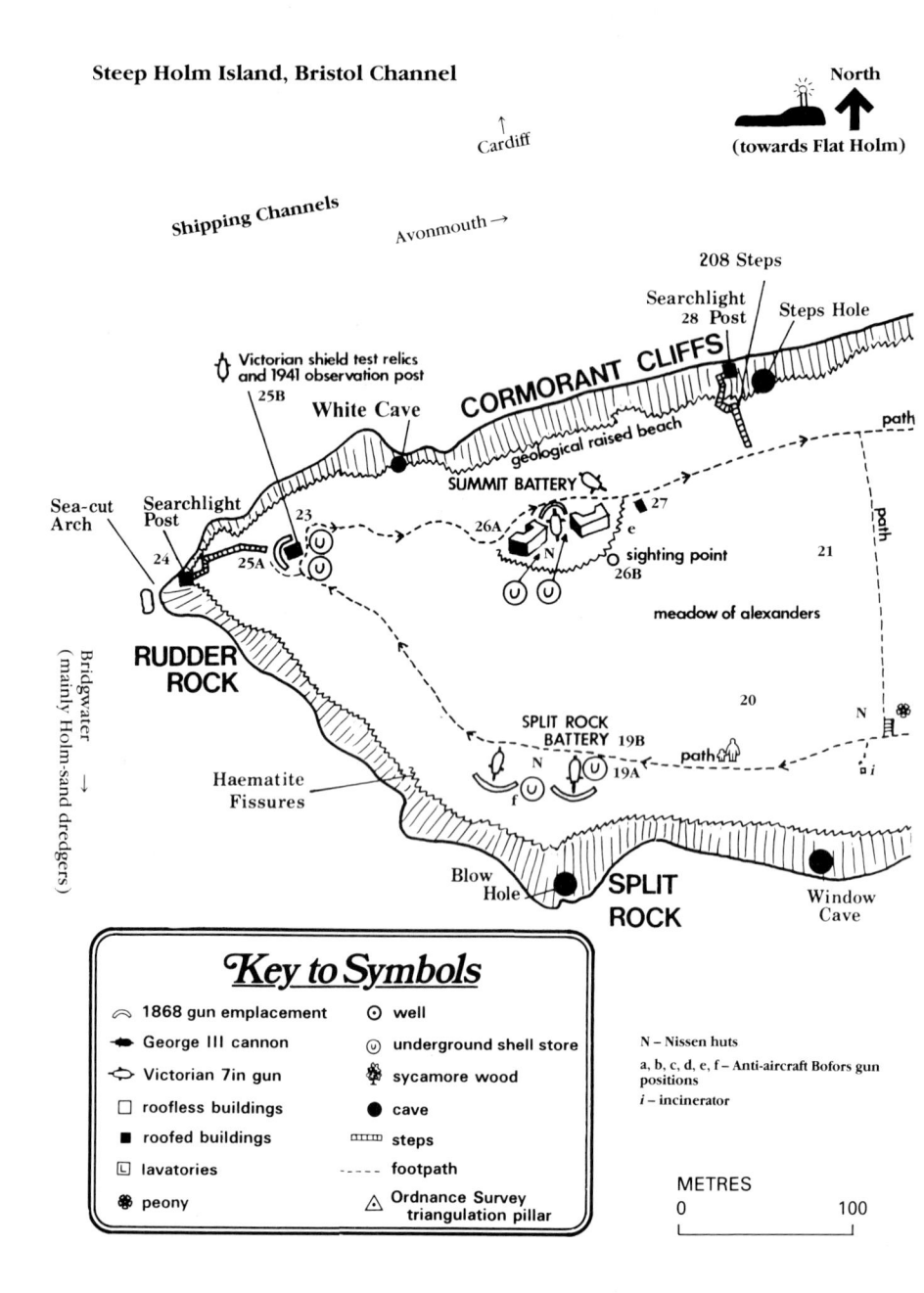

Steep Holm Island, Bristol Channel

↑ Cardiff

North
(towards Flat Holm)

Shipping Channels
Avonmouth →

208 Steps
Searchlight 28 Post
Steps Hole

Victorian shield test relics and 1941 observation post
25B
White Cave
CORMORANT CLIFFS
geological raised beach
path

SUMMIT BATTERY
27
Sea-cut Arch
Searchlight Post
23
26A
e
24
25A
sighting point
26B
21
path

meadow of alexanders

RUDDER ROCK
20
N

Bridgwater (mainly Holm-sand dredgers)

Haematite Fissures

SPLIT ROCK BATTERY 19B
19A
path
i

Blow Hole
SPLIT ROCK
Window Cave

Key to Symbols

- ⌒ 1868 gun emplacement
- George III cannon
- Victorian 7in gun
- ☐ roofless buildings
- ■ roofed buildings
- Ⓛ lavatories
- ❋ peony

- ⊙ well
- ⓤ underground shell store
- sycamore wood
- ● cave
- ⊞ steps
- ----- footpath
- △ Ordnance Survey triangulation pillar

N – Nissen huts
a, b, c, d, e, f – Anti-aircraft Bofors gun positions
i – incinerator

METRES
0   100

This map is from the 1985 edition of Rodney Legg's book **THE STEEP HOLM GUIDE**. The numbers have their entries in that, but there have been updatings, such as the addition of number **34**, namely **Parsons Cave** which is a rounded cavity two metres high and 2.5 metres deep. Its main interest is that it had been walled up in the eighteenth or early nineteenth centuries, probably as a smuggling hideaway, and has been named for its 1985 discoverer - Tony Parsons, the Crewkerne veterinary who has chronicled the island's wildlife and is himself seen in characteristic plumage on page 95.

As for the symbol of the 24-pounder George III cannon, **26C** has moved from Summit Battery to the Barracks. That event took place on 25 September 1986, courtesy a Sea King helicopter of 707 Naval Air Squadron, and the gun barrel was winched down to a wooden carriage constructed by Ken Cass. John Pitfield then stuffed it with a pound of gunpowder and fired a wooden shell seawards at 400 mph, which splashed down half a mile south of the island, being recovered by John Watts in the **Weston Lady**. That may sound like wanton disturbance to the birds but the spectacular daily antics of Tornadoes and other war-planes make them blasé about the odd little bang.

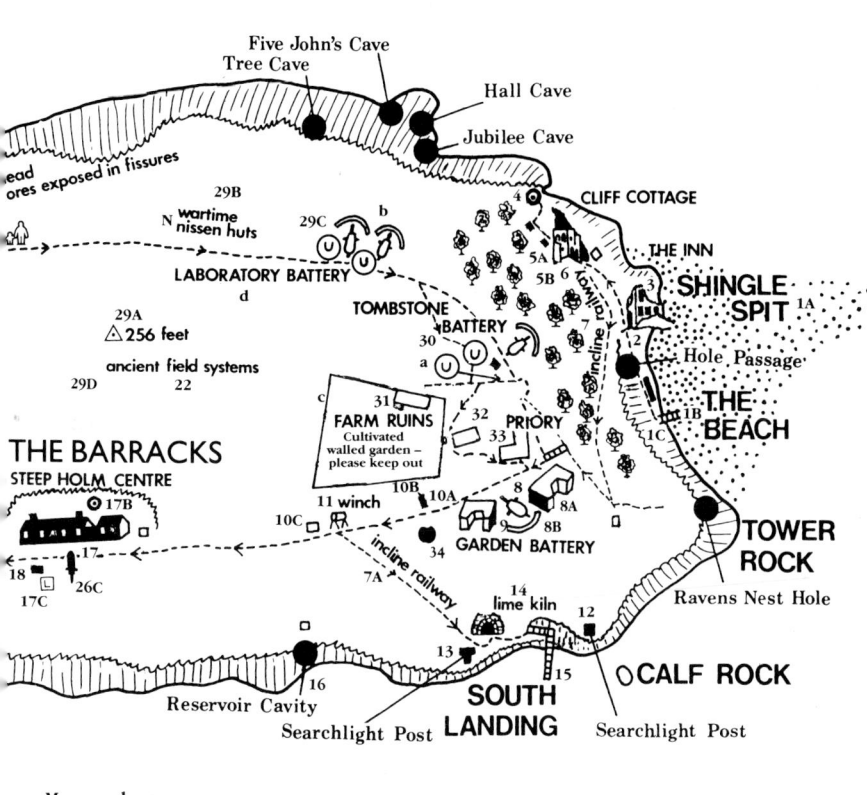

Map numbers

1A	Stakes for nets	10C	Generator house	24	Searchlight post
1B	Beach landing	11	Railway winch	25A	Rudder Rock Battery
1C	Bristol boundary stone	12	Searchlight post	25B	Battery Observation Post
2	Telephone exchange	13	Searchlight post	26A	Coast Defence Battery
3	Inn/Warden's depot	14	Limekiln	26B	Coast Defence Battery
4	Monks' well)	15	Jetty	26C	Georgian cannon
5	Cliff or Smugglers Cottage	16	Water-haul	27	Generator house
5A	Water tank bases	17	Steep Holm Centre/Barracks	28	Searchlight post
6	Allsop plaque	17B	Water tank	29A	Triangulation pillar
7	East cliff railway	17C	Latrines	29B	Latrines
7A	South Landing railway	18	Boundary stone	29C	Laboratory Battery
8	Garden Battery)	19A	Split Rock Battery	29D	Water & fuel tank bases
8A	Coast Defence Battery	19B	Latrines	30	Tombstone Battery
8B	Range-finding point	20	Cultivation terraces	31	Farmstead/"Garden Cottage"
9	Coast Defence Battery	21	Field boundaries	32	Tenement ruin
10A	Generator house	22	Field boundaries	33	St Michael's Priory
10B	Limekiln	23	Boundary stones	34	Parsons Cave

Manx Shearwater: too many of these and we won't sail (see page 6).

Steep Holm

Basic Details

Country: England
Location: middle of Bristol Channel, downstream from the Mouth of the Severn.
County: Avon (detached); Somerset (detached) before 1 April 1974.
District: Woodspring
Parish: none (not part of any civil parish)
Ordnance Survey map reference: ST 229 607 is a six-figure reference to the central plateau. Eight-figure references follow for some of the key landmarks.

    Rudder Rock (sea-cut arch) ST 2243 6065
    Summit Battery (west emplacement, built 1941) ST 2262 6069
    Split Rock Battery (west barbette, built 1867) ST 2266 6057
    208 Steps Searchlight Post (built 1941) ST 2274 6078
    Barracks (built 1867, centre door) ST 2288 6060
    Triangulation pillar (256 feet) ST 2291 6072
    Ruin of Augustinian Priory ST 2314 6066
    Inn Ruin (being rebuilt by the author, 1983 to 1993; the grid reference is to the incorporated Royal Artillery Telephone Exchange, built 1941) ST 2320 6073
    Tower Rock (outcrop) ST 2323 6062

Latitude: 51 degrees 20 minutes north
Longitude: 3 degrees 6 minutes west

Nearest land: Flat Holm (sister island) — 2 miles north-north-west. Brean Down (promontory, Somerset) — 3 miles east-south-east. Northward — Cardiff (mud) Flats, South Glamorgan, 9¼ miles. Southward — Stolford, near Hinkley Point Power Station, Somerset, 9 miles. Eastward — Beach Lawns, Weston-super-Mare, Avon, 5¼ miles. Westward — Goose Cove, Newfoundland, 2,800 miles.

Size: 48.87 acres above high-tide level and expanding to 63.26 acres at mean low water.

Shape: Oval, 825 metres (east to west) by 315 metres (north to south), and extending to 1,230 metres by 360 metres at low tide. In profile the island rises to a domed plateau, reaching 78 metres above the high water mark.

Tidal range: Considerable, its rise varying from a minimum of 8 metres above low water to a maximum 13 metres in height, this extreme being caused by the funnelling effect of the narrowing estuary.

Geology: Lower Carboniferous Limestone, 330 million years old, the same basic formation as Brean Down and the Mendip Hills.

Statutory protection: Site of Special Scientific Interest, designated by the Nature Conservancy Council. Special Protection Area under the European Commission Bird Directive.

Ownership: Kenneth Allsop Memorial Trust Limited; registered charity number 270059. Conserved by the Trust since 1974, with purchase of the freehold being achieved in 1976, as a memorial to naturalist and multi-media man Kenneth Allsop [1920-73].

Access: By booking with the Trust, its ferry generally operating from Knightstone Causeway, Weston-super-Mare, on Saturdays and bank holiday Mondays when weather and tides allow (usually leaving either 90 minutes before high water, or 90 minutes after high water). For a copy of the current sailing programme and the Trust membership details send a 241 x 165 mm stamped addressed envelope to the Kenneth Allsop Trust, via Wincanton Press, National School, North Street, Wincanton, Somerset BA9 9AT.

Further information: The Trust has published reports and magazines with natural history records collected by Tony Parsons. Rodney Legg has written several books about the island. Additional findings and updatings are always appreciated and can either be handed over at the Trust's sales counter on the island or posted to the mainland address given above.

Birds

Nota bene:
Sequence follows the standard ornithological practice.

Fulmar: coming to stay.

- **Fulmar** Probably will breed, if they have not already done so, as several birds have been noted at various times between April and October in recent years. The species has had a steadily expanding range since it spread from Shetland at the end of the nineteenth century.

- **Manx Shearwater** Since our trips to the island began in 1973, Colin Graham and I always pretended to ignore the implications of seeing Manx Shearwaters clipping through the waves. They are our birds of ill omen because they portend bad weather. Their arrival is a few hours ahead of a storm. The record for the island was the 45 that Tony Parsons noted on 6 June 1977: "The weather was appalling with heavy cloud, high wind and rain squalls, and it is likely that many more than this passed during the day."

☐ **Gannet** Rare visitor, though when one comes it will often stay for a week or two.

☐ **Cormorant** Generally between forty and sixty pairs in the colony along the north-western cliffs. They breed early in the year and on 17 April 1977 Tony Parsons found one nest had fledglings — an exceedingly early date for a British nest to have young. The young are flying by the end of June. The birds stay on the island throughout the year though they fly considerable distances to fish. Steep Holm has the only Cormorant cliffs in the Bristol Channel.

Cormorant: after the gulls, this is the island's commonest seabird. It is present all year and breeds on the northern cliffs.

BIRDS, page 7

Cormorants: seen above and on the island,
plus an inevitable Herring Gull beside one of the nests.

BIRDS, page 9

Heron: unlikely to land, for those that approach soon realise there is a problem with air traffic control.

Shelduck: this 'prettily marked species', to use Thomas Bewick's words, is the island's most common duck and frequently flies out from its nesting areas on the eastern cliffs as a boat comes toward the landing beach.

☐ **Heron** It is probably about once a week that a Heron coming or going from the Somerset Levels makes the mistake of coming too close to Steep Holm. Once it is in the gulls' air space a considerable commotion follows, even at night, and the harassment is violent. The Herons usually gain height in an attempt to escape the close interceptions by a mass of Herring Gulls and frequently they are disorientated from their flight-path in the process.

☐ **Canada Goose** Rare visitor, the only record so far being a flock of nine that settled on the sea in front of the Barracks on 3 June 1986.

☐ **Shelduck** Between ten and twenty pairs normally breed on the dense canopy of ivy that smothers much of the eastern cliffs. They bring off their week-old chicks to tumble down into the sea in June though one wonders at the overall success rate thereafter given the choppy and changeable nature of these waters and their abnormal tide-flow.

☐ **Mallard** There are usually two to four pairs around the island and most years there is proof of at least one pair having bred. An early flock of more than twenty was present off the beach on 12 February 1989.

Mallard: present all year, with occasional winter flocks and usually at least one pair that stays on the island to breed.

☐ **Eider** Rarely sighted, usually after severe weather. Seven were off the island on 31 May and 12 June 1979, and could well have been off course due to a deluge on 30 May.

BIRDS, page 11

page 12, BIRDS

Shelduck: on the water, in and out of the egg, and in the arms of Jenny Smith.

BIRDS, page 13

☐ **Common Scoter** Occasionally pass by, usually being spotted from the boat, such as on 1 August 1987 when two males and a female were seen a mile east of the island.

☐ **Long-tailed Duck** Seen rarely; an immature female was on the sea off South Landing, with Shelduck, on 16 May 1987.

☐ **Sparrowhawk** Regular spring and autumn visitor. Because of their low flying bush-height interceptions of small birds they are liable to netting by the ornithologists. After many near misses Tony Parsons was able to put rings on to two of them in 1986.

☐ **Buzzard** Occasional sightings when a bird tries to over-fly the island, at height, and is intercepted by a multitude of gulls. Sometimes a Peregrine will join the mobbing. Once the ferocity of the attacks grounded a Buzzard on the top of the island.

Buzzard: big target for gull attack, which once succeeded in grounding an intruder.

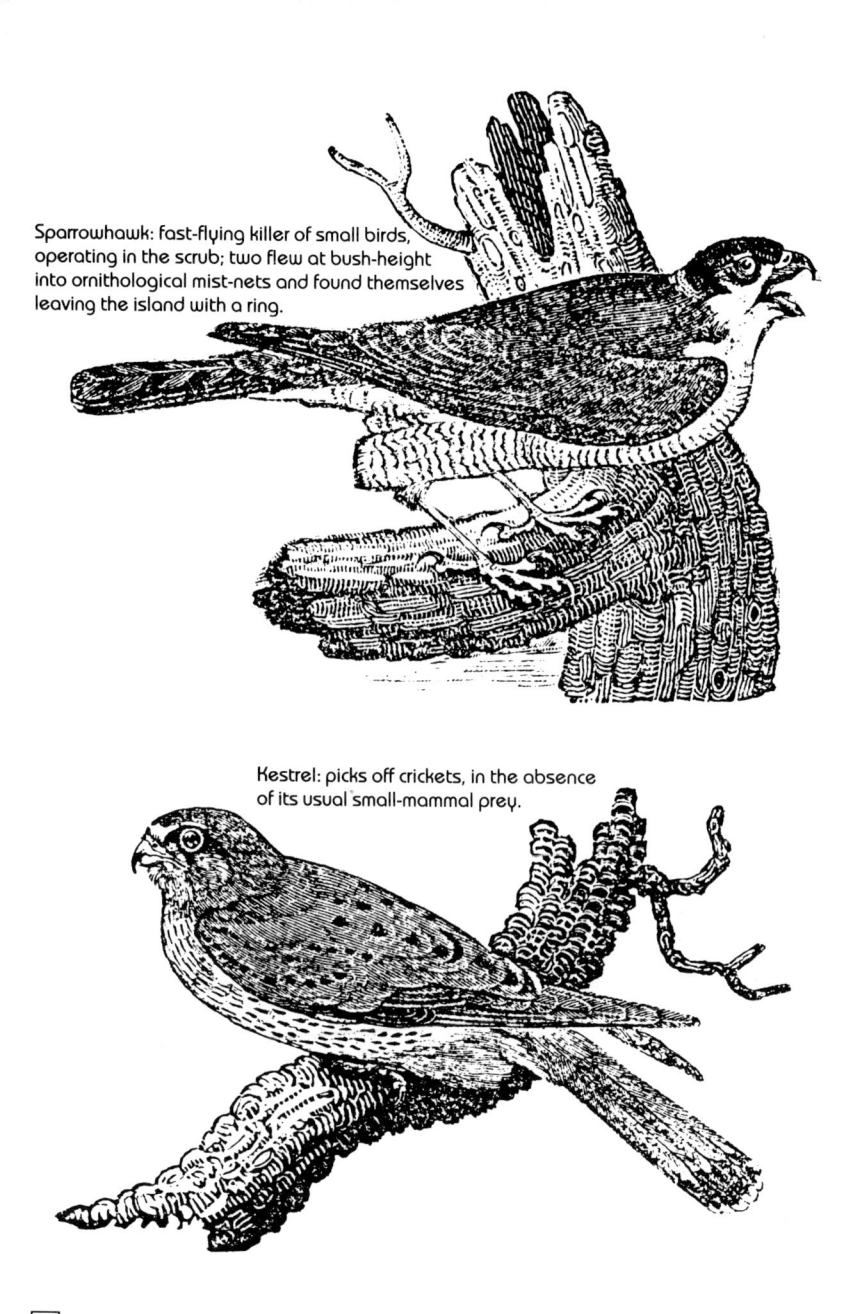

Sparrowhawk: fast-flying killer of small birds, operating in the scrub; two flew at bush-height into ornithological mist-nets and found themselves leaving the island with a ring.

Kestrel: picks off crickets, in the absence of its usual small-mammal prey.

☐ **Kestrel** Frequent post-breeding visitor, generally only a single bird, in late summer and autumn. That they are sometimes around for so long is, perhaps, surprising as the island has no small mammal

BIRDS, page 15

prey, but the scrub of the southern slopes is sometimes teeming with Dark Bush-crickets. These must have sustained the two Kestrels that were present on the island for most of September and October in 1982.

OPPOSITE — Peregrine: the island's Pigeon-fancying predator par excellence, in a post-Bewick drawing, by Victoria Oakley.

Merlin: 'smallest of all the Hawk kind, scarcely exceeding the size of a Blackbird', Bewick writes. They follow the migrating Swallows.

☐ **Merlin** Occasional spring and autumn visitor. They follow the migrants and though the island records have yet to yield such a perfect sighting I had to do an emergency stop for one, on my way to Steep Holm for an April visit, when it brought down a Swallow on the road beside the Castle of Comfort on the Mendip Hills. The first spring sighting for the island came on 2 April 1983.

☐ **Hobby** Rare spring and autumn visitor.

page 16, BIRDS

☐ **Peregrine** Present all year and generally one pair manages to breed in an eyrie on the cliffs. The breeding location has tended to move and the young are airborne by July. Seaward "key-key-key" flights of parental protest normally signify disturbance by naturalists as the birds are generally accustomed to the island's normal visitor flow patterns. Kills are frequently brought down by the Peregrines on paths, rocks, and even the middle of the Boathouse floor. The most exciting and unexpected moment of my life came in 1982 when I was building at the Inn and a whoosh of a Peregrine stoop split the air. By the time I looked up the falcon had levelled seawards and a Pigeon lumbered erratically up-Channel. You can't win them all.

On 15 October 1988 the *Weston Lady* arrived off Steep Holm at about 9.30 am in a sharp north-easterly wind which had waves breaking over the beach-side boathouse. It soon became clear that we would be unable to land but whilst the boatmen pondered the situation we noticed two Peregrines. A male bird was virtually hanging in the air, facing into the 18 miles per hour wind, about thirty feet above the highest point of the sycamore wood. Meanwhile a much larger female bird shepherded a small flock of starling-size birds, about two dozen, harassing them in a circuit from the top of the wood at Tombstone Battery, across to Tower Rock and then northwards along the lower edge of the tree cover to Cliff Cottage.

That was where we left them, the flock in panic and constantly trying to put into the trees, at which moment the female Peregrine swept alongside to drive them out again. The intention seemed to be to force them seaward so that the male could single out a target and stoop.

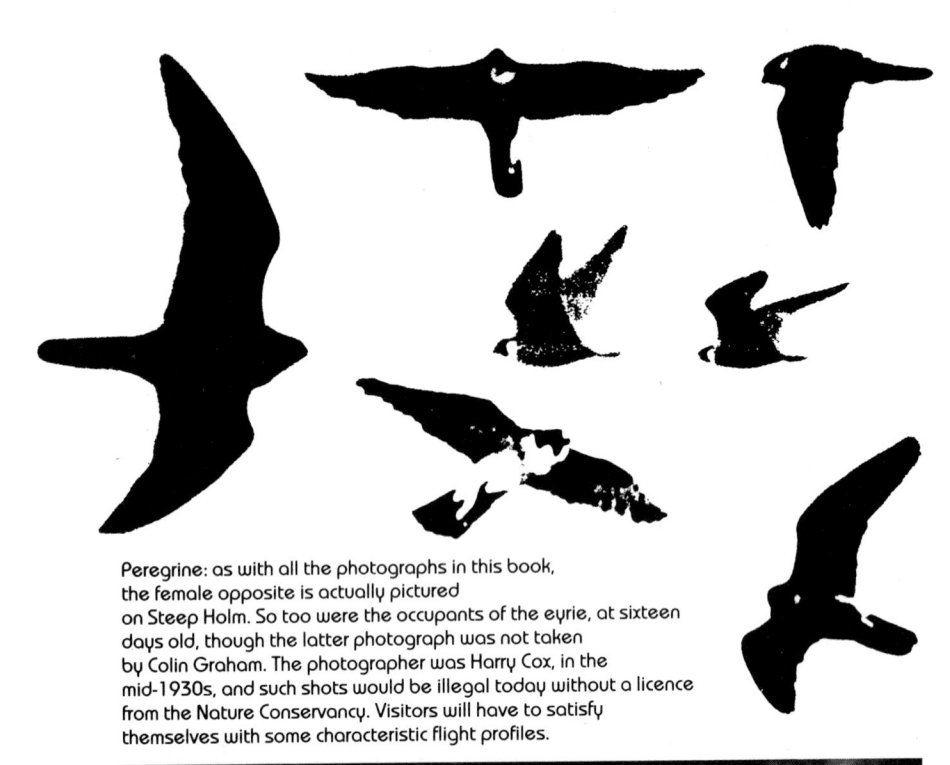

Peregrine: as with all the photographs in this book, the female opposite is actually pictured on Steep Holm. So too were the occupants of the eyrie, at sixteen days old, though the latter photograph was not taken by Colin Graham. The photographer was Harry Cox, in the mid-1930s, and such shots would be illegal today without a licence from the Nature Conservancy. Visitors will have to satisfy themselves with some characteristic flight profiles.

page 18, BIRDS

BIRDS, page 19

Pheasant: introduced to Steep Holm in 1981 by Barry Westwood, who brought some further birds the following summer. An initial population explosion was followed by years of poor breeding and numbers stabilised. Some fine specimens are likely to be seen, and certainly heard.

☐ **Pheasant** Introduced in 1981-82 and breeding, with variable results. An initial population explosion has been followed by lower, stable numbers in the region, probably, of twenty pairs. The summers with a high breeding success have been those with hot dry weather and high numbers of insects, such as 1984, when one of the nests contained fourteen eggs. That year there were many young scurrying for cover beside the paths but in damp seasons few chicks have been seen.

Oystercatcher: frequent tide-line visitor, most often sighted from the former beer-garden at the Inn.

☐ **Oystercatcher** Regular visitor, particularly in the second half of the year, generally at low tide when a small flight of three to five birds will work its way around the rocks from the Inn to Split Rock.

☐ **Ringed Plover** Rare late summer visitor, generally occurring only as a solitary bird flying over.

☐ **Golden Plover** Occasional autumn visitor. On 6 October 1986, Tony Parsons watched six approach the island from Wales and he thought they were preparing to land, but then "one of the charges being used to clear Summit Battery exploded and they changed their minds".

☐ **Lapwing** Occasional visitor, usually only a single bird.

☐ **Purple Sandpiper** Occasional, as in 1979 when there was one off Rudder Rock on 12 May and four below Tower Rock on 13 May – Gerald More was able to approach within six yards of them.

BIRDS, page 21

Dunlin: common wintering wader of the Severn Estuary, which is a wetland of international significance.

☐ **Dunlin** Occasionally feed on the mud on the north side of the shingle spit when this is exposed by a particularly low tide. Chris Woodfield and Tony Lewis counted a flock of 91 there on 9 August 1979, following a night of gale-force northerly winds. In putting forward the Severn Estuary as a Ramsar Site – a wetland of international importance – the Nature Conservancy Council said it was among the ten most important estuaries for wading birds in Britain and "especially significant for dunlin, supporting over ten percent of the British wintering population".

☐ **Woodcock** Rarity. The only recorded specimen is that which I flushed out of dense Alexanders on the top of the island on 12 May 1979, giving a shock to both it and me.

☐ **Whimbrel** Occasional sightings, usually single birds flying up the estuary as on 19 May 1979.

☐ **Curlew** Occasionally, most often at low tide in the late evening, the cry of a Curlew can be heard from the Inn as it flies over the shingle spit.

☐ **Common Sandpiper** Rare sightings, usually one to five birds, at low tide.

☐ **Turnstone** Occasional single-figure movements up or down the Channel.

page 22, BIRDS

☐ **Arctic Skua** Seen rarely, usually from the boat, such as the immature bird spotted flying towards Weston on 19 March 1985.

☐ **Black-headed Gull** Occasional visitor, small flocks being seen in transit.

☐ **Lesser Black-backed Gull** Breeds with the Herring Gulls on the cliffs, and is frequently seen perching in elder trees on the southern slopes of the island. There are generally between two hundred and three hundred pairs.

☐ **Herring Gull** The commonest of the island's breeding birds with somewhere around a thousand pairs. This is well down on the vast numbers that were reached in the mid-1970s when there was a population of 6,500 pairs nesting on the island, and though the decline might have been accentuated by drought years and disease it has certainly been maintained by the use of plastic rubbish sacks which have greatly diminished the quantity of mainland tip-food that is available for scavenging. They depart the island for the winter, feeding on inland fields, and return to establish nest sites in February. These are mainly on cliff ledges and slopes but some always occur in a wide variety of alternative locations, including paths, buildings, amongst Alexanders, and even beneath the sycamore trees. Eggs hatch in April-May and the young become airborne in July-August. Immature birds then tend to congregate off the beach and virtually the entire population exits from the island in September.

Herring Gull: protesting human disturbance.

BIRDS, page 23

Herring Gull:
on nest, the eggs
and emerging young.

OPPOSITE — Lesser Black-backed Gull:
perching on an Elder tree.

page 24, BIRDS

BIRDS, page 25

Great Black-backed Gull: showing its giant wing-span as it glides from an outcrop, and a chick on the cliff edge, beside a Tree Mallow plant.

Great Black-backed Gull: this species, Thomas Bewick writes, 'is the largest of the tribe'.

☐ **Great Black-backed Gull** These are the great gulls of the outcrops. Though they appear to co-habit with the smaller Herring Gulls it is a situation that changes when the chicks are born. Simon King photographed a Great Black-backed Gull pick off and kill a flightless young Herring Gull when he was filming on Steep Holm in 1986. Unlike the other gulls, the Great Black-backed tend to restrict their choice of nest-site to the exposed tips of the outcrops, such as Tower Rock and Rudder Rock, where they can lift off in a broad sweep over the sea. There are generally between fifteen and twenty pairs nesting on Steep Holm.

☐ **Kittiwake** Occasional visitor, generally when a flock of twenty to fifty birds sweeps past the island.

☐ **Sandwich Tern** Rare sightings, as they fish off the island or fly past the beach.

☐ **Common Tern** Occasionally seen in the autumn in small numbers, with parties up to a dozen.

BIRDS, page 27

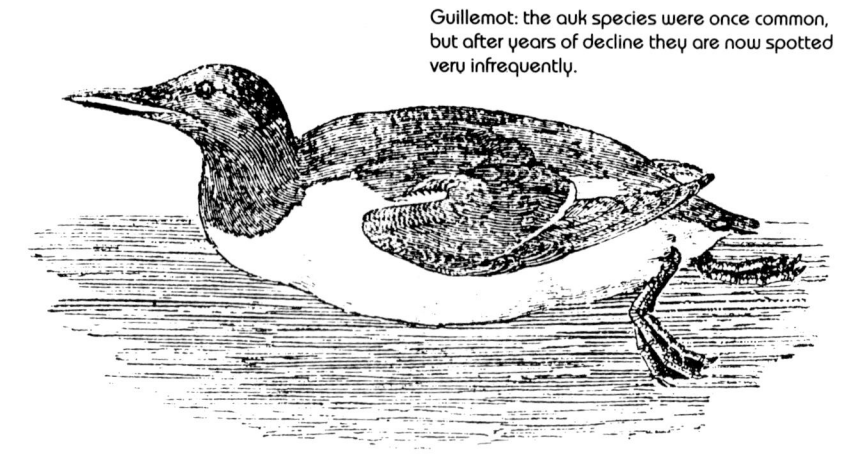

Guillemot: the auk species were once common, but after years of decline they are now spotted very infrequently.

☐ **Guillemot** Occasional visitor, though as with the other auks the sightings in recent years have tended to be only isolated specimens moving up or down Channel.

☐ **Razorbill** Rare visitor, usually only as a single bird since auk numbers have declined all around the western shores.

Turtle Dove: the bird in the bush on 20 August 1978 then found itself in the hand as Tony Parsons put a ring on its leg.

☐ **Stock Dove** Breed regularly on the cliffs, formerly to the extent of eight to ten pairs, and there seems to have been some interchange of population with Flat Holm. Numbers on both islands dropped during the 1980s as the birds provided Peregrine-pickings.

☐ **Wood Pigeon** Regularly bred on the island, with up to three pairs being the norm in pre-Peregrine days, but it is now an endangered species as far as Steep Holm is concerned.

☐ **Collared Dove** Occasional sightings, with one of a flock of seven singing in the sycamore wood in the spring of 1978, but any thoughts of breeding would have been reversed by the return of the Peregrine.

☐ **Turtle Dove** Rare visitor; one was present all day on 20 August 1978 when it was successfully trapped and ringed.

☐ **Cuckoo** Occasional spring returnee, even to Steep Holm, though most years it probably goes unheard.

Short-eared Owl: sightings of any owl are extremely rare.

☐ **Short-eared Owl** Rare visitor; one hunted over the north-eastern part of the plateau on 10 October 1982.

BIRDS, page 29

Nightjar: the only specimen recorded on the island left wearing a ring, its dawn emergence from the Alexanders at Garden Battery having coincided with the unfurling of a mist-net.

☐ **Nightjar** Rare autumn migrant. The first to be recorded in the island was a lucky early morning find for ornithologist Tony Parsons who spotted the juvenile emerging from the Alexanders at Garden Battery on 26 August 1977 and propelled it into the net he was in the process of unfurling.

☐ **Wryneck** Occasional autumn visitor. One spotted below Split Rock Battery on 4 October 1980 conveniently flew into a mist net and was ringed later that afternoon.

Swift: almost constantly on the wing, the high-flyer of the summer skies.

☐ **Swift** Occasionally fly over the island in the spring and summer; seldom noted during the autumn migration.

☐ **Green Woodpecker** Rarely sighted, with the exception of a male that spent at least seven weeks around the north-east corner of the island in August-September 1983. He apparently fed on ants, in the considerable amount of dead sycamore wood still rotting from the 1976 drought.

Skylark:
a few are generally
around during the autumn.

☐ **Skylark** Frequent autumn migrant, but usually only half a dozen at a time.

☐ **Sand Martin** Occasional spring and autumn migrant. Numbers generally are small, in the region of a dozen birds, but up to fifty have sometimes been seen in September and October.

☐ **Swallow** Fly north up the Channel in April, as well-spaced parties of a dozen to twenty at a time. In the autumn small numbers sometimes stay around the island for several days, from August to October. Several thousand a day regularly pass over in the September mass-movements.

☐ **House Martin** Spring and autumn migrant with sporadic April sightings and mass movements of several hundred at a time in September and October. The heaviest passages tend to be after a coastal fog has held up their migration and then lifts to allow them to fly. Sometimes the mist comes down again and traps House Martins along with a selection of other passerines, on Steep Holm for the night or longer.

☐ **Tree Pipit** Occasional autumn visitor but only individual birds are normally sighted.

☐ **Meadow Pipit** Regular visitor in the spring and autumn migrations. Some of the latter passages can be heavy, such as that

BIRDS, page 31

between 25 September and 4 October 1986 when more than 2,250 crossed the island and a substantial proportion landed for a time.

☐ **Rock Pipit** Regularly breeds on the northern cliffs and occasionally on the eastern and southern slopes as well. There are generally around five pairs on the island.

☐ **Richards Pipit** Rarity on Steep Holm as it is nationally; the island's single specimen being that which Tony Parsons spotted over Tombstone Battery early on 17 September 1979 and recognised immediately, "being a large, dark, streaked pipit with a characteristic sparrow-like call".

☐ **Flave Wagtail** Sometimes seen in April and May and then spotted again in the autumn migration, from August to October, though usually only in single-figure numbers.

☐ **Grey Wagtail** Occasional autumn visitor, usually with only a single bird being sighted.

☐ **Alba Wagtail** Occasional spring and autumn visitor, sometimes with largish numbers of a hundred or more being seen in September and October.

☐ **Wren** Common and sometimes abundant, particularly after a mild winter and in and around the ivy-covered eastern cliffs. Some fifteen to twenty-five pairs breed most years. Numbers built up considerably in 1981, when Tony Parsons ringed 46 of them but of ten found dead in one place in the Barracks after the 1981-82 winter none had been ringed. Hopes that the island population was insular and might become a sub-species were dashed on 18 July 1982 when a Wren was killed by a cat at Créteil, in the suburbs of Paris. The bird was ringed by Tony, as a Steep Holm juvenile, on 16 August 1981.

☐ **Dunnock** Usually the commonest small bird on the island. The population is remarkably stable and seems to average between thirty and forty pairs. Their contribution to ornithological research came in 1963 when Ray Poulding noticed, and demonstrated for the first time, how they could be aged from changing iris colour. This sequence is now used by ringers. The work was made possible by the fact that the Dunnocks of Steep Holm have a closed population, resident on the island and independent of the mainland.

☐ **Robin** Present most years with up to a dozen pairs breeding. Common as an autumn visitor.

☐ **Redstart** Regular spring and autumn visitor, usually in small numbers.

Wren: denizen of the ivy on the eastern cliffs,
but not with a closed island population — which became
a proven fact when a Steep Holm migrant was caught by a Paris cat.

Dunnock: on the other hand the Dunnock, the commonest of the island's small birds, does maintain an insular population. Studies of this species on Steep Holm led to the discovery by Ray Poulding of a system for ageing the birds from their iris colours.

BIRDS, page 33

☐ **Whinchat** Occasional spring and autumn visitor. A juvenile male was caught and ringed on 2 September 1984.

☐ **Stonechat** A rare spring and autumn visitor.

Wheatear: this little bird returns to enliven rocky cliffs during the migration months.

☐ **Wheatear** Regular spring and autumn visitor usually as solitary birds.

☐ **Ring Ouzel** Occasional spring and autumn migrant. Usually only single birds are spotted.

Blackbird: common, conspicuous and noisy, this is likely to be the first of the smaller birds that you will spot on the island.

☐ **Blackbird** Among the island's commonest smaller birds. There are usually between twenty and thirty breeding pairs and sometimes apparent post-breeding seasonal influxes of additional birds from the mainland.

☐ **Fieldfare** Occasional autumn and winter visitor, such as on 22 October 1983 when at least twenty were present, and ten were seen on 5 November that year.

Song Thrush: there are a few resident pairs of this songster, and a plentiful supply of snails and rocks on which to hammer them.

☐ **Song Thrush** A small population is maintained on the island. Probably the number is usually between five and ten pairs. The bird can look particularly colourful to human eyes when it is about to crack open one of the island's multi-banded snails.

☐ **Redwing** Occasional autumn migrant, generally represented by single birds but sometimes small flocks descend on the island.

☐ **Mistle Thrush** Occasional sightings of individuals, such as on 12-13 October 1978 and 19 September 1985 when single birds were present all day.

☐ **Grasshopper Warbler** Occasional autumn visitor. Some years a bird will stay on the island for a month or more. Prefers the eastern scrubland.

☐ **Lesser Whitethroat** Occasional autumn visitor. Two were ringed in 1978.

☐ **Whitethroat** Occasional autumn visitor with isolated specimens in the main.

☐ **Garden Warbler** Regular autumn visitor though generally in only small numbers. Two were ringed on 28 September 1981.

☐ **Blackcap** Proved breeding, which is probaby occasional, though it is regular as an autumn visitor.

☐ **Sedge Warbler** Occasional autumn visitor, an adult being trapped and ringed in the eastern scrub on 18 August 1981 and a juvenile caught nearby on 29 September.

☐ **Yellow-browed Warbler** Occasional autumn visitor though it was not until 27 September 1986 that the first was ringed – and then trapped again the following day.

☐ **Wood Warbler** Rare visitor, and perhaps sometimes resident. In 1984, for example, one was singing in the sycamore wood on 19 May – only the second record for the island – and a sighting was made in the same area on 29 September.

Firecrest: naturalist parson Francis Blathwayt predicted in 1906 that the Firecrest would one day be caught on the island. Veterinary ornithologist Tony Parsons would prove him right with this autumn specimen in 1975, and in 1984 the first spring record followed.

☐ **Chiffchaff** Occasional spring and summer records, though no evidence of breeding. Regularly passes through in the autumn with steady passages of substantial numbers of birds.

☐ **Willow Warbler** Regular spring and summer migrant with occasional midsummer records though no proof of breeding. Only light numbers are generally seen on passage.

☐ **Goldcrest** An autumn migrant, sometimes in quantity, but its movements tend to be variable in date and number.

☐ **Firecrest** Regular autumn visitor. The first spring record was made in 1984 when a male was singing from a sycamore tree on 19 May. Twelve Firecrest were ringed on Steep Holm between 1975-87. One was retrapped eighteen months later on the Suffolk coast, a location that indicated such visitors may be of continental rather than British origin.

☐ **Spotted Flycatcher** Occasional records from April to October but no proof of breeding.

☐ **Pied Flycatcher** Regular sightings from April to September but no evidence of breeding.

☐ **Coal Tit** Generally a rarity, the exception being the autumn migration in 1985 when upwards of sixty were present in the first week of October and fourteen were ringed.

☐ **Blue Tit** Regularly seen in the autumn migration and occasional summertime sightings, but most years they do not appear to breed on the island.

☐ **Great Tit** Occasionally resident, with apparently the same male being reported on 5 May and from 19 May to 2 June 1984. One was ringed on 2 September that year.

☐ **Magpie** Normally breed on the island and family groups have been seen though so far there has been only a single nest per year. This is usually in the sycamore trees below Tombstone Battery.

☐ **Jackdaw** One or two pairs usually breed on the northern cliffs in the vicinity of 208 Steps. There are occasional autumn influxes of parties from the mainland though these seldom stay very long.

☐ **Carrion Crow** Frequently breeds on the island; usually a single pair in the sycamore wood.

☐ **Raven** Present on the island throughout the year since one pair bred, very early in 1986, on the cliffs to the west of South Landing.

Tony Parsons considers they probably take gull chicks, a view reinforced when he saw a Raven intercepted by Herring Gulls over the island, and croaking in utter distress as it found itself with attackers hanging on to both wing-tips. Young Ravens are also attacked by the gulls. Sometimes they are also harassed by Peregrines, as on 18 December 1988 when an adult was disturbed by human visitors from its territory at South Landing. It flew towards Summit Battery, turning to croak at the people as it came over the Barracks, and then found itself in close combat with a Peregrine which made several swoops at it.

Raven: 'the largest of this kind', writes Thomas Bewick; 'its length is above two feet, breadth four'. A pair generally nest on the west side of South Landing.

☐ **Starling** There used to be a major roost in the sycamore wood, with numbers building up during the summer of 1977 from 7,500 on 27 August to in excess of 10,000 by 28 October. Sometimes a dense black swarm of birds, swirling into the sky, gave rise to reports from the mainland that the island was on fire. By 1986, the numbers had

Jackdaw:
a couple of pairs
nest on the north
cliffs, and are
usually seen
in the vicinity
of 208 Steps.

Magpie: a pair generally nest
in the Sycamores immediately
beneath Tombstone Battery.

dropped to occasional small flocks of twenty to fifty birds, and Tony Parsons witnessed the reason: "On at least two occasions, on 15 and 18 June, the male Peregrine attacked a Starling flock approaching from Flat Holm direction."

☐ **Chaffinch** Regular autumn visitor though usually only in smallish flocks, below fifty, in September and October.

☐ **Brambling** Occasional autumn visitor, generally only as single birds. Sometimes amongst a flock of Chaffinch as on 11 October 1978.

BIRDS, page 39

☐ **Greenfinch** Bred regularly on the island in the 1970s, though with only one or two nests, but no recent records of breeding or even a summertime presence. Regular autumn visitor.

☐ **Goldfinch** Rarely sighted in the spring migration but occasional in the autumn, usually in small flocks though movements upwards of 160 were recorded on 11 October 1978, a month when 11 were ringed.

Siskin: distinctive, with black-topped head and yellowish-green underparts that bring splashes of autumn colour to the island.

☐ **Siskin** Regular autumn migrant. Some years, as in 1985, its numbers increase into a noticeable influx.

☐ **Linnet** Migrant which passes through the island in the autumn. Massive flocks, upwards of a thousand, have been recorded.

☐ **Redpoll** Occasional autumn visitor, generally only single birds or the sighting of a small flock, though in 1984 there were larger movements – up to 32 at a time.

☐ **Yellowhammer** Occasional visitors, generally in autumn and in small numbers.

☐ **Reed Bunting** Occasional autumn visitor, generally in small flocks.

☐ **Cockatiel** Rare, unfortunately, though the proximity of the South Wales conurbation does provide scope for occasional such exotic escapees. One spent the afternoon on the island on 19 September 1982.

Mammals

Rabbit

☐ *Oryctolagus cuniculus* (Rabbit). As in Britain as a whole the rabbit is the wild animal one is most likely to see on Steep Holm, but as I have catalogued in my book on *Steep Holm Legends and History* it was once an extreme rarity and an island speciality. The Steep Holm colony dates from the original continental imports to Britain during the time of the Plantagenet kings. The animals were a valuable commodity, particularly for their fur on the western islands and for food when they were kept nearer the country's eastern population centres, and they were warrened on the island by the twelfth century Augustinian canons and their secular successors – until rabbits made their escape from managed confinement on islands, promontories and enclosed burrows into the English countryside as a whole.

That process took several centuries; it was not until the 1840s that the rabbit had expanded its range to cover all England. The Steep Holm colony, as I have documented in the other book, retains a distinct reddish cast and is the pure-bred form of the imported rabbit brought from continental Europe in Plantagenet times.

Its island isolation proved to be no protection, however, from a much later, Franco-Australian organism. The myxoma virus *Myxomatosis cuniculus* arrived on the island in 1955, having been deliberately introduced, according to Dorothy Crampton of the former Steep Holm Trust. Myxomatosis did not arrive on Lundy until 1983, when it was accidentally brought by rabbiters. Locally and nationally the initial fatality level was as near total as anyone could measure – the experts settled for 99 percent.

Equally amazingly the pandemic did not reduce the rabbit's coverage of the country or even take-out isolated extremities of its range, such as Steep Holm or the Farne Islands. I have compared notes with naturalists from there and found that in both cases recurrent crashes in rabbit population kill off 90 percent of the animals but leave a healthy minority that breeds just as is expected of the proverbial rabbit and restores a full population in two or three years. Then the disease hits again.

Hedgehog

☐ *Erinaceus europaeus* (Hedgehog). The hedgehogs of Steep Holm are descendants of those introduced to the island in 1975. They are the standard English kind, picked up on main roads in north Dorset as they came out of hibernation, and are different only in that they are without their usual companion, the flea *Archaeopsylla erinacei*. All six had been treated with flea powder, effectively it seems.

In 1977 there was "an apparently massive increase in the number of hedgehogs on the island" and Tony Parsons dissected fifteen faecal casts to establish whether there had been predation on the slow-worms. Fortunately his conclusion, that year and in later studies, was negative, and most of the animals also ignored the island's abundant woodlice and snails. Only two of the samples contained traces of these. Six faceas had fragments of ground beetles and six the remains of centipedes. The outright gourmet winner was the earwig with between two and twenty-three individuals having found their way into twelve of the fifteen samples. The twenty-three earwig cast was nothing else: "This latter sample apparently contained nothing but the remains of earwigs, and raises an interesting point. There would appear to be individual preferences shown by some hedgehogs, but it could well be that the hedgehog is purely an opportunist, taking advantage of whatever ready supply of food is handy."

Five faeces were studied in 1978, with similar results, though two contained Devil's Coach-horse Beetles and another the large weevil *Othiorhynchus clavipes* which was only the second record for this species on the island. There was evidence from the droppings that the hedgehogs had congregated, as Konrad Herter has recorded in Berlin parks, with the mass assemblies on Steep Holm having taken place on the gull-lawn above the Barracks and a sandy slope below Split Rock Battery.

Then, from late summer in 1978 through to the late 1980s, hedgehog numbers slumped into a decline from which they never recovered. There were a number of fatal mishaps, such as the huge male that stuck his head into a tin of Marvel milk-powder on the rubbish chute, and one that drowned in the Monks' Well, but most of the corpses appeared to be scattered at random. The cause of that sudden drop may well be natural balancing after an initial population explosion. A few individuals could have ingested type C botulism from gull corpses, which the birds generally pick up from rotting vegetation at the water's edge, but this is a toxin rather than a contagious disease. Cold winters are likely to have taken a much greater toll, particularly of the younger animals.

There may be a shortage of places for hibernation, though in the mild 1988-89 winter that was of little concern to the island's hedgehogs. Fresh droppings were found in January and a healthy half-grown male encountered at Summit Battery on the night of 12 February 1989.

Muntjac deer

☐ *Muntiacus reevesi* (Muntjac). The Muntjac of Steep Holm are, like the rabbit, an introduced species not just for the island but for England too. They have travelled somewhat further. "Springing and graceful" their name means, in the dialect of the Sundas, the string of tropical Indian Ocean islands off the coast of Sumatra. The general form of the English species seems to be that of *Muntiacus reevesi*, which is named after John Reeves [1774-1856] who was an inspector of tea with the East India Company in Canton. Britain has also seen imports of *Muntiacus muntjak*, the Indian strain, which is said to be more aggressive. They may well have inter-bred and merged into the current wild population.

The eleventh Duke of Bedford [1858-1940] brought the Indian species to his park at Woburn in the period 1872-1900. The animals are so small and fast, having the size and speed of a fox, that escapes were inevitable. By the 1930s they were also escaping from Whipsnade and Wormley Bury in Hertfordshire. Christopher Lever has charted the animal's feral progress in *The Naturalised Animals of the British Isles*, into a range that covers most of central and south-eastern England, and puts its success down to "being unobtrusive, secretive, and causing only limited damage" which "draws scant attention to its presence, and its antlers provide only a meagre trophy for the sportsman".

The animal was introduced to Steep Holm in January 1977 with four healthy specimens which had been netted in a wood beside the A1 road in Hertfordshire. There was an unfortunate imbalance of sexes, one female and three males, which could have ended the animals' presence. Muntjacs tend to develop family groups, rather than herds, and drive off young bucks. Where these find no escape, as on Steep Holm, they are known to corner a female and have sex with her until she is dead.

On Steep Holm there was an additional problem. Amanda Allsop's prophetic words in 1977 had been: "Won't they fall off?"

Muntjac sometimes venture down to the sea for salt. This applies

Muntjac: January 1977 and the release of number two, a male, into the Alexanders of Steep Holm.

particularly to the males, probably because minerals are essential for antler growth, and has led to a series of misadventures. The safest route to the rock pools is via the steps to the South Landing but a more precipitous course is to travel the slanting undercliff from the eastern cliffs to the sloping shelf beneath Tower Rock. Landslips are frequent in this area and one was triggered by a family of Muntjac, a pair with a baby, that crashed down to their deaths a hundred feet below. In the winters of 1984-85 and 1985-86 at least seven Muntjac were killed in accidents of this type; it is the most common cause of mortality and keeps the island herd to about twenty animals.

Surplus males are said to have a tendency to worry the females and can cause a cornered individual considerable distress. This may also tend to scare animals into dangerous areas. It was also inevitable that an expanding population would cause territorial pressures on the deer to migrate into less favourable habitat. To compound this the

Muntjac is not a herd animal — however much I like referring to it as "the herd" — but is a collection of pairs and families that appear to be strictly territorial. When parted they become extremely agitated and bark, very much like a dog, to regain contact.

Muntjac: January 1977 and the release of number four, also a male, to a farewell stroke from author and warden Rodney Legg. His apologies for the cropping of boatmen's heads, but this is all that appears on the photograph. 'Rodney's wretched pets', John Fowles would call the deer, in the subsequent controversy over island introductions, which is documented in the book, 'Steep Holm — Allsop Island'.

The first known fatality, to one of the original four, occurred on the evening of 22 September 1978. The unfortunate male, who was already lame, slipped from the eastern cliffs and fell on to the beach. When we arrived on the next tide, in the morning, the carcase was examined by veterinary surgeon Tony Parsons. As with most Muntjac sightings, its general body-weight and appearance were good, and later full post-mortem examination found no external or internal parasites. It did, however, have a lame foot and an abdominal rupture and intestinal prolapse that had all resulted not from the final fall but from a lesser accident of about a month before.

The stomach contents included a largish frond of bladder wrack, and several smaller pieces of seaweed, which indicated it was returning from the shore. There were also the odd leaves of nettle and bramble and unidentified fragments of other plants.

The bulk of the stomach contents were the fruits of the island's two principal scrub-species which were ripe at the time. There were over 500 privet berries and considerable amounts of foliage that had been eaten at the same time. More that 2,000 elder seeds showed that elderberries had also been consumed in quantity though this time the foliage had been avoided as no leaves were found that could be positively identified as elder.

The coat was a beautiful russet, the colour and sheen of a conker, and his size was about average for this small browsing species. The length from the tip of the nose to the end of the tail was 85 cm. The weight was 8.6 kilograms.

The worst single calamity to befall a Muntjac family occurred in about February 1984 when a male and female and a 1983-born male dropped to their death in a rock-fall a hundred feet above the boathouse at the eastern end of the island. There was a visible scar near the top of the cliffs where a section of limestone, amongst a tangle of ivy, had broken away. A track churned with deer-slots led into this otherwise impenetrable mass of dense scrub, as indeed it does once more at the end of the decade, but even with this loss and a poor number of sightings there are indications that the colony survived. At the end of the hot summer of 1984, members of Timsbury Natural History Group observed that many of the elder bushes across the top of the island had a distinct browse line that was higher than the rabbits could reach.

Though Alexanders are shunned, the deer are partial to Tree Mallow, a cliff-growing maritime species. The mild winter of 1988-89 provided its best growing conditions for years and a small forest of deer-height plants appeared around the Quay in January 1989. By 12 February this had been intensively grazed rather than browsed, with every plant in an area of several square yards being levelled to an inch stump. Not only had their removal been systematic and precise, without leaving any mess, but the deer had desisted from touching the adjoining stands of Tree Mallow, apart from occasional leaves that projected into the cleared zone. They are remarkably orderly eaters.

Orkney Vole

Cardiff chemist Robert Drane visited Steep Holm on 25 May 1907, with others from Cardiff Naturalists' Society, and released six of the Orkney species of vole. He noted in his diary that *Evotomys orcadensis* was a "new and northern species" and looked forward to the surprise of someone happening to find it on Steep Holm. They didn't; the introduction was unsuccessful.

Bats

☐ *Pipistrellus pipistrellus* (Pipistrelle). This is the only common bat on Steep Holm, as indeed it is throughout much of Europe, and it seems they are still breeding in the Barracks and, probably, Five Johns' Cave and some of the other cavities along the northern cliffs. They sometimes roost elsewhere and one unfortunate specimen, hanging beneath the old beach ladder, was camouflaged by its dusky-brown coat when the time came to creosote the steps.

They are the smallest of Britain's bats and are generally active from about an hour after sunset. Their prey species, airborne insects, are generally more prolific along the warmer southern side of the island and most bat sightings are in that area.

Grey Seal

☐ *Halichoerus grypus* (Grey Seal). The seals that are seen from Steep Holm, and its ferry boat, come up from the Pembrokeshire breeding grounds and follow the salmon run into the upper Bristol Channel. They are generally common, from July onwards, in periods of calm weather. There is not much future in trying to fish around Steep Holm at other times and unfortunately there is no suitable haul-out on the island. Neither the beach nor any of the accessible ledges stretches for a usable distance above the high-tide mark.

So it is only in fishing that the seals can be observed. They are most often seen around the shingle spit off the beach, because there the fish congregate into a small volume of water to cross the shallows. A more dramatic view is to look down, and catch the attention of their dog-like heads, from Split Rock. There the interception is of the fish that have turned left instead of right upon reaching the island and are heading around the western rocks.

Porpoise

☐ *Phocoena phocoena* (Porpoise). The smallest cetacean, the porpoise is up to 1.8 metres in length and has low, blunt lines. The body is plump with a small low fin and a rounded beakless snout.

They were once as commonplace as the paddle-steamers but disappeared together from the western shores. Schools of them used to venture into British inshore waters each summer but now only occasional small parties are sighted. One such group, of only two or three, took a passing interest in the *Weston Lady* as she sailed homeward a mile east of Steep Holm, on the evening of 25 July 1987.

Slow-worms

☐ *Anguis fragilis* (Slow-worm). The distinctive fact about many of the Steep Holm reptiles, its slow-worms, is that they are bluish. Most adult males are covered with blue spots, across the upper parts of their bodies, and particularly on the dorso-lateral series at the demarcation line between the light colour of the back and the heavier (though often bluish-black) markings of the underparts. This coloration is not apparent in young slow-worms but begins to appear during the third year of their lives.

The author of *The British Amphibians and Reptiles*, Malcolm Smith, claims the blueness occurs only in males. Far from being recorded only in Steep Holm Slow-worms, it was first described by A. de Demidoff in 1840 from the eastern shore of the Russian Black Sea at Port Euxin. The blue strain on Steep Holm continues into the 1990s, with examples up to sixteen inches in length, and more bluish than

Slow-worm: what's missing? The animal has a tail but David Wilson should have put a coin beside his find, to substantiate the claim that this fine specimen was in excess of 500 mm. in length. That would beat the British record.

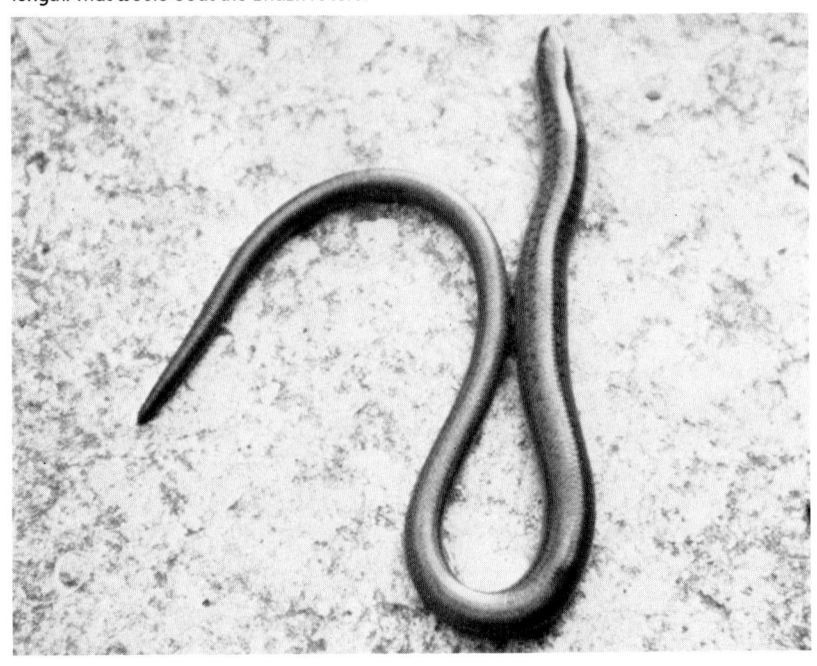

Slow-worm: female and young, from Thomas Bell's 'History of British Reptiles', published in 1839.

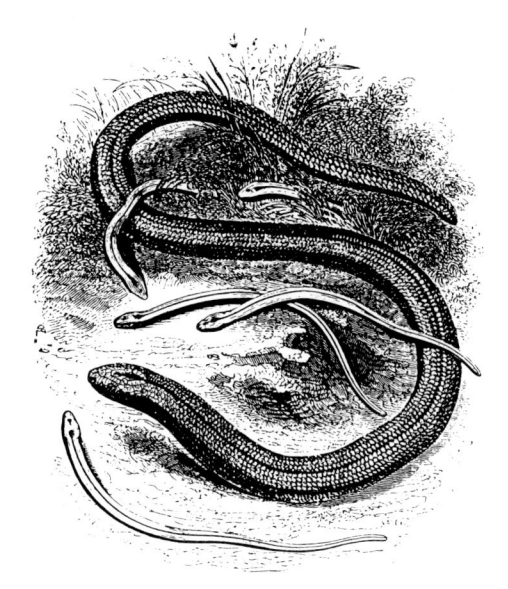

grey, being seen in both 1976 and 1977, and a record-breaking specimen removed for study in 1984.

It is difficult to estimate quite how common the Slow-worm is on Steep Holm. There must be between 500 and 1,000, if not more. Generally, through the summer, basking animals are reported every fortnight, and sometimes the claims are astounding, like that of the International Voluntary Service team in 1975 who, even under persistent questioning, refused to withdraw the statement that they had found an animal one metre in length. It would be the longest Slow-worm ever discovered outside continental Russia, and whatever its true size, it has entered island folklore. In most other cases at that time, gulls had grabbed the animal's tail, showing that many more must have been gobbled head first. As gull numbers declined, the incidence of tail loss also dropped, but this came too late for most of the best specimens.

One bluish male, eighteen inches long but with only a stumpy tail, was found in 1975 by Tony Phelps, who was working at the time on reptiles for the Nature Conservancy at Furzebrook in Dorset. He estimated it was between sixty and seventy years old. Had he taken the individual back he could have claimed the British record.

Indeed, a similar specimen from Steep Holm holds the national record for a tail-less Slow-worm. It was found by Jenny Smith, as it lay semi-curled beside the path from the Tenement to the Farmhouse, on 19 May 1984. I made a grab for it but let go in fear of causing

SLOW-WORMS, page 49

damage. Nick Smith, from Southampton University, happened to be on the island to study its rather special Slow-worms. Jenny and I took him to the spot and the creature was miraculously back in place. Nick, as sportsmen say, made no mistake and it was in his hands. "This is the sort of size you find in Hungary," he said.

Even without the tail it was the heaviest ever recorded from the British Isles. It had a snout to vent length of 250 mm, plus a reduced (second) tail of 141 mm. The weight was 60 grams. Had it not lost its first tail the overall length would have been about 530 mm (instead of 391 mm) and easily in excess of the existing 489 mm British record holder.

As with many other of the male Slow-worms on the island it had two rows of vivid blue spots along its back that had merged into a continuous colour band down each side.

The dependable way of finding Steep Holm Slow-worms is to lift rusting pieces of Second World War ironwork but though this can often provide a couple of examples it also disturbs the habitat on which they depend for survival. It is impossible to replace corrugated iron precisely as it was found – Timothy Eden please note – or to be completely sure you are not tramping across other Slow-worms, or that your disturbance is not about to scatter young animals.

Slow-worms occur on Lewis and other islands in the Outer Hebrides, as they do on the Shetland Islands and, off Wales, Anglesey, Bardsey and Flat Holm. They are absent from Ireland, from which they must have been eliminated by the last ice-age, though there is every reason to think that reintroductions would do well. Returning to the Steep Holm blueness, Malcolm Smith observes that such colour may "vary from light Cambridge blue to deep ultramarine". The general Steep Holm colour seems to be the former, an overall mid sky-blue, and it is only through the observation of marked or captive animals that we will know whether his secondary observation – that "the colour is not constant: the blue may disappear at any time, leaving a brown spot in its place" – applies on the island.

Slow-worms have been recorded on Steep Holm for many decades, their distribution in recent years ranging from dense scrub at the centre of the island to batteries on the cliff edge and youngsters beside the ruins of the Inn but isolated, older reports that the island has adders and common lizards have never been substantiated. Wall lizards might seem a more appropriate reptile for the island's geography and climate, but the ban on further introductions prevents these being brought across.

Invertebraes

Banded Landsnail: Victoria Oakley's drawing shows one of its multiplicity of designs, though some have none at all and are just a single colour.

Banded Landsnail

☐ Dr Cuillin Bantock, a population geneticist working at the Polytechnic of North London, spent a week on Steep Holm in 1972 studying the banded landsnail *Cepaea nemoralis*. He concluded that these were larger and more colourful than those of mainland populations, and that the size and marking ratios of the island snails were related to its southern-oceanic climate. The temperature of this microclimate has since been measured by Peter Tailby as an average five percent higher than mainland values by day and rising, because of the heat-retention of the sea, to ten percent higher at night.

Bantock's argument, however, is of an environmental cause that has given rise to snail growth that is "chromosomally different" and he proceeded to prove this by taking batches of Steep Holm snails to a series of cages in the grounds of the Leonard Wills Field Study Centre at Nettlecombe on Exmoor.

Here the snails duly continued to breed with the unusual island characteristics. Another factor in shell size, which is "greater than on both Flat Holm and the nearest point on the mainland" is that the banded landsnails of Steep Holm have been spared any significant predation. Charles Darwin's studies of island fauna hit upon that correlation, that the easing of predation leads to larger animals, but Bantock's observations were the first to apply the rule to banded landsnails.

There is, however, predation upon snails on Steep Holm. The Song Thrush population is quite noticeable, and there are occasional traces of snails eaten-out from the rear in hedgehog fashion, though hedgehogs had not been introduced to the island in 1972. What on the other hand was then much larger than in the 1980s was the gullery. Considerable quantities of landsnail shells are sometimes found gathered like trophies around nests.

Slugs

For most of the time slugs are relatively uncommon on the island but ☐ *Deroceras reticulatus* and ☐ *Arion hortensis* occur. The limiting factor seeems to be the general dryness of Steep Holm but when the climate decides otherwise, as in the spring of 1986, their numbers multiply.

Woodlouse

☐ It is possible that as with the banded landsnails the woodlouse of Steep Holm can grow to a size several millimetres beyond the maximum set in the national keys. That discovery was made by Dr Cuillin Bantock as an aside from his research on the snails but he never returned to investigate the woodlice more thoroughly. Hugh Boyd studied them in 1949 but did not draw attention to abnormal sizes.

In the 1980s, Tony Parsons found a number of localised populations of pink woodlouse, *Androniscus dentiger*, under scree and beside ruins at the damper eastern end of the island.

Purse-web Spider: and its home, which is the condom-like tube, displaced from under a rock.

Purse-web Spider

☐ The remarkable Purse-web Spider, *Atypus affinis*, has delighted John Fowles and other naturalists but will not draw itself to the attention of most visitors. An estimated 5,000 live in the scree slopes above Calf Rock, and probably similar numbers beneath the Barracks and at Split Rock on the cliffs that slant at 30 degrees towards the sun, but they are well concealed.

What makes them interesting is that they live sealed into silken tubes that are between six inches and two feet in length. Much of this will be buried. The spider has fangs and waits for its prey to land on the innocent-looking dirty outer surface of the tube. Then it strikes to immobilise the prey and draws the victim through the membrane and down into the larder, in the dark bottom of the tube, and the spider immediately returns to repair the damage caused in the process. Then it will eat.

Culvert Spider

☐ One interesting continuing inhabitant of the underground magazines at the gun batteries, and in the cave systems, is the Culvert Spider, *Meta menadri*. This species, a relative of the orb-web spinners common to every garden, is strongly photophobe, or light-shunning. Its charming white egg-sacs, like Japanese lanterns, hang from every magazine roof. The underground stores are also used by hibernating butterflies and moths, though eventually most probably become contributions to the spiders' food supply.

Jumping Spider

☐ The Jumping Spider, *Heliophanus cupreus*, is reasonably common on the southern cliffs. It is one of nature's acrobats and leaps on to prey.

Banded Spider

☐ Spiders are among the wildlife that develops differently in closed island communities. This was proved with *Enoplognatha ovata* on 22 August 1981. The species shows wide colour variations, with about a quarter of mainland specimens being banded. On Steep Holm, however, the incidence was much higher. Of the one hundred examples collected, 48 were banded, 46 yellow, 3 mixed colours, 2 pink, and the remaining one seems to have fallen by the wayside. Portland, Dorset, shows a similar banded majority but on Lundy the proportion drops to 17.5 percent. The tendency with islands is for a predominant type to emerge, though as the figures show this can be either of the majority mainland type or the one that is the minority elsewhere.

Rare Spiders

Two of the many species of spiders recorded from Steep Holm are rare in national terms. Neither has an English common name. Both are specialised coastal species and the squat ☐ *Oxyptila blackwalli* is shaped like a miniature toad.

☐ The other, the six-eyed *Segestria bavarica*, is restricted to rock-crevices just above the splash-zone. It is common along the half-mile band of southern cliffs but, like many of the spider species, it is not generally found on the colder northern cliffs.

Butterflies and Moths

Large numbers of butterflies can suddenly appear on Steep Holm. Most will be migrants, and there is a frequent movement of insects from Brean Down in particular, but some are born and stay to hibernate on the island, both in natural scree slopes and man-made cavities such as the underground shell and cartridge stores.

Usually the most abundant are the Small Tortoiseshell, Red Admiral, and Peacock. Large White and Small White swarms are also common, almost always as immigrants, as are most of the attractive Painted Lady, though some emerge here. Sometimes the island is touched by a rarity two Channels removed, such as when there was a continental influx of Clouded Yellow to Britain in 1984.

Red Admiral:
on a Teasel.
Butterflies migrate
in quantity and sometimes
hundreds descend upon the island.
The Red Admiral also breeds here,
though some years it has been
almost completely absent, as in 1981.
Then it featured in a political
joke. 'Where are the Red Admirals?'
'They've gone to the Baltic.'
Solidarnosc was being crushed in Poland.

As for moths, the ☐ Silver Y-Moths are common immigrant swarms, but very much home-grown — to the extent some years of consuming every bramble, hawthorn and fruit-tree leaf on the island — is the red and black striped ☐ Lackey Moth.

Speckled Wood: orange-brown spots of the British sub-species of this butterfly, in a dappled pattern that camouflages it in the woodland fringes. It breeds on Steep Holm and the larvae feed on the coarser grasses.

Rarities include a ☐ Lime Hawk-Moth found by Dave Reid on 28 August 1982 beside the path at Split Rock, and the coastal ☐ Feather Ranunculus found in the Barracks on 11 October 1982.

Of the 59 butterflies on the British list, 19 were recorded from Steep Holm in the period 1976-88: ☐ Clouded Yellow, ☐ Brimstone, ☐ Large White, ☐ Small White, ☐ Green-veined White, ☐ Orange Tip, ☐ Small Copper, ☐ Common Blue, ☐ Holly Blue, ☐ Red Admiral, ☐ Painted Lady, ☐ Small Tortoiseshell, ☐ Large Tortoiseshell, ☐ Peacock, ☐ Comma, ☐ Speckled Wood, ☐ Wall Brown, ☐ Gatekeeper, ☐ Meadow Brown.

Hoverfly

☐ Sometimes there are masses of hoverflies over the island, from May to September, and in one year alone – 1985 when their numbers happened to be much lower than usual – Tony Parsons identified eighteen species.

Dragonflies

The spectacular migrating insects are the dragonflies. They are liable to move in some numbers across the Bristol Channel on delicate warm afternoons in September and October. It needs to be a good insect year, following a hot summer, for there to be large numbers – say a dozen to fifty alighting in the sheltered Garden Battery area in the course of a couple of hours – but even in lesser numbers they tend to be noticeable.

Green, yellow and blue ☐ Southern Aeshna, *Aeshna cyanea* is the usual arrival but some years there have been occasional sightings of much rarer species, for instance a female ☐ Golden-ringed Dragon-fly, *Cordulegaster boltoni*, on 4 October 1986.

Green-bottle

☐ The Green-bottle, *Lucilia sericata*, is the commonest fly on the island though as with dung-beetles it does not do so well now that gull numbers have slumped from their peak in the mid-1970s.

Blue-bottles are also abundant, particularly the ☐ Red-headed Blue-bottle, *Calliphora vicina*.

Seven-spot Ladybird

☐ One of the insect phenomena of the century took place in the drought years of 1975 and 1976 when the air was thick with swarms of the Seven-spot Ladybird, *Coccinella septempunctata*. They settled all over the island, the beach, and in wide rafts out at sea. As we arrived back at Weston-super-Mare one evening we found a similar coating on Birnbeck Pier. The vast majority had flown into the area rather having been born on the island or anywhere else in the locality.

There are, however, island residents as larva of the ☐ Seven-spot Ladybird were found feeding on a colony of thistle aphids, *Brachycaudus cardui*, on a ragwort plant in July 1986.

Common Field Grasshopper

☐ There are small numbers of the Common Field Grasshopper, *Chorthippus brunneus*, on Steep Holm. They are sometimes relatively frequent along short stretches of path but the general lack of long grass is probably the factor limiting larger numbers.

Speckled Bush-cricket

☐ The green Speckled Bush-cricket, *Leptophyes punctatissima*, is another long-legged species. It is like the Dark Bush-cricket in all but colour and sound. The latter is subdued, as it strigulates virtually inaudible series of chirps, and is seen rather than heard. It is common throughout the scrub-belt along the southern side of the island.

Dark Bush-cricket

☐ Omnipresent in the Steep Holm night throughout the autumn is the Dark Bush-cricket, *Pholidoptera griseoaptera*, which maintains a cacophony of intense chirrups. It is brown with long legs, and the female has extended curved ovipositors.

Frog Hopper

☐ A bright-green denizen of the scrub is the little Froghopper, *Philaenus spumaris*, which is common from midsummer into the autumn.

Devil's Coach Horse

☐ A largish carrion beetle that was exceedingly common on Steep Holm at the time of the great gullery, and less so since numbers of both live and dead gulls have fallen, is the Devil's Coach Horse, *Ocypus olens*. It is visually as good as its name. Not only is it black with a segmented body but it has the scorpion-like habit of turning its abdomen as if to strike the intruder – harmless but disconcerting.

"Oh, what a horrible creepy-crawly!" Pauline Yesson exclaimed as she looked down beside the Barracks stove in 1977. "That's no creepy-crawly," four-year-old Lucy Parsons corrected her, "That's a Devil's Coach Horse beetle."

Lesser Cockroach

☐ The Lesser Cockroach, *Ectobius panzeri*, was recorded from Steep Holm in 1938. This particular species, however, is a panzer of the shoreline rather than the kitchens. If it still has a population on the island this would be the upper extremity of its range along the Bristol Channel as it is not recorded east of Carmarthen and North Devon.

Harvest Mite

☐ An island late-summer speciality is the reappearance of the Harvest Mite, *Trombicula autumnalis*, on just about anything warm blooded that it can find. That includes, on Steep Holm, almost every Blackbird and Dunnock – one of the latter, trapped for ornithological ringing in August 1976, carried 500 mite larvae, but despite that seemed quite healthy. Rabbits, hedgehogs, Muntjac and long-stay humans have their quota.

Tony Parsons, a veterinary surgeon, says "the tiny orange-red larva" penetrates the upper layers of skin and that the irritation is intense: "The best antidote is to swab the affected areas with methylated spirit, and the only consolation is that most of the irritation will have subsided in twenty-four hours."

Rabbit Flea

☐ The Rabbit Flea, *Spilopsyllus cuniculi*, is the vector in the transmission of the deadly myxomatosis virus.

Flora

Sequence follows the standard botanical format.

Polypodiaeceae (Fern family)

☐ *Osmunda regalis* (Royal Fern). First noted 1979 with a single clump in a damp ledge on the north-east cliff, east of Laboratory Battery, but no recent record.

☐ *Phyllitis scolopendrium* (Hart's-tongue Fern). First noted 1883 and common on the eastern and north-east cliffs.

☐ *Asplenium adiantum-nigrum* (Black Spleenwort). First noted 1883 and probably occasionally found on the eastern cliffs, though no record since 1977.

☐ *Asplenium trichomanes* (Maidenhair Spleenwort). First noted 1883 but no recent record.

☐ *Asplenium marinum* (Sea Spleenwort). First noted 1773 and frequent on the cliffs.

☐ *Asplenium ruta-muraria* (Wall Rue). First noted 1831 but no record since 1967.

☐ *Ceterach officinarum* (Rusty-back Fern). First noted 1923 but no recent record.

☐ *Dryopteris filix-mas* (Male Fern). First noted 1966 with a single large clump in a drainage gully on the north side of the Barracks, which was unfortunately destroyed during clearance work in about 1980.

☐ *Polyodium vulgare* (Polypody). First noted 1831 and common on the eastern and northern cliffs.

☐ *Polypodium interjectum* (Shivas). First noted 1969 and occasional on the northern cliffs.

Ranunculaceae (Buttercup family)

☐ *Anemone nemorosa* (Wood Anemone). First noted 1883 but no recent record.

☐ *Clematis vitalba* (Traveller's Joy). First noted 1883 but no recent record.

☐ *Ranunculus acris* (Meadow Buttercup). First noted 1883 and occasional on northern cliffs.

☐ *Ranunculus repens* (Creeping Buttercup). First noted 1883 and found again in 1977 at Garden Battery. It is now present annually around the eastern end of the island.

☐ *Ranunculus bulbosus* (Bulbous Buttercup). First noted 1891 and occasional on the eastern cliffs.
☐ *Ranunculus arvensis* (Corn Crowfoot). First noted 1965 but not subsequently.
☐ *Ranunculus sardous* (Hairy Buttercup). First noted about 1980 and flourishing in the Farmhouse ruin until, in the words of Tony Parsons, "somebody put half a ton of rock on it".
☐ *Ranunculus sceleratus* (Celery-leaved Crowfoot). First noted 1965 and occasional at Garden Battery until clearance work apparently caused its extinction.
☐ *Ranunculus ficaria* (Lesser Celandine). First noted 1883 but no recent record.

Paeoniaceae (Peony family)

☐ *Paeonia mascula* (Wild Peony). First noted 1803 and occasional, with a natural clump on eastern cliffs and gardened specimens west of Barracks and at the Priory. Probable monastic introduction and the only naturalised colony of this plant in the British Isles that has a mediaeval pedigree.

Wild Peony: single flower blooms, but still spectacular, drawn by Victoria Oakley.

FLORA, page 59

page 60, FLORA

Wild Peony: the island's floral speciality, in full flower
and with the subsequent pod bursting to reveal black fertile seed.
Packets of these are offered for sale by the Kenneth Allsop Trust
in the hope that visitors will desist from stealing their own.

FLORA, page 61

Papaveraceae (Poppy family)

☐ *Papaver dubium* (Long-headed Poppy). First noted 1891 and occasional, particularly around Laboratory Battery.

☐ *Papaver somniferum* (Opium Poppy). First noted 1977, "from deliberate scattering of seed", and since eradicated by gull and human intervention.

☐ *Chelidonium majus* (Greater Celandine). First noted 1965 and occasional on the eastern cliff, usually beside path.

Fumariaceae (Fumitory family)

☐ *Fumaria capreolata* (Ramping Fumitory). First noted 1890 but no recent record.

☐ *Fumaria officinalis* (Common Fumitory). First noted 1883 but no recent record.

Cruciferae (Cabbage family)

☐ *Brassica oleracea* (Wild Cabbage) First noted 1837 but doubtful.

☐ *Brassica napus* (Rape/Swede group). First noted 1891 but no recent record.

☐ *Brassica rapa* ssp. *campestris* (Bargeman's Cabbage, now generally known as Rape). First noted about 1836 and common on top of the island and the northern cliffs; the plant species that visitors most frequently ask me to identify.

☐ *Sinapsis arvensis* (Charlock). First noted 1883 but no recent record.

☐ *Diplotaxis muralis* (Wall Rocket). First noted 1891 but no recent record.

☐ *Diplotaxis tenuifolia* (Perennial Wall Rocket). First noted 1891 but no recent record.

☐ *Raphanus maritimus* (Sea Radish). First noted 1883 and found again in 1988.

☐ *Cakile maritima* (Sea Rocket). First noted 1883 but no recent record.

☐ *Lepidium campestre* (Field Pepperwort). First noted 1883 but no recent record.

☐ *Coronopus squamatus* (Procumbent Swinecress). First noted 1963 and occasionally found on the cliffs.

☐ *Coronopus didymus* (Lesser Swinecress). First noted 1964 but no recent record.

☐ *Capsella bursa-pastoris* (Shepherd's Purse). First noted 1891 and occasional on the cliffs.

☐ *Cochlearia officinalis* (Common Scurvy-grass). First noted 1883 and occasional on the lower cliffs.

☐ *Cochlearia danica* (Early Scurvy-grass). First noted from before 1688 but no recent record.
☐ *Erophila verna* (Common Whitlow-grass). First noted 1890 but no recent record.
☐ *Cardamine hirsuta* (Hairy Bittercress). First noted 1883 and occasional on the eastern cliffs.
☐ *Barbarea vulgaris* (Winter Cress). First noted 1883 but no recent record.
☐ *Cheiranthus cheiri* (Wallflower). First noted 1883 and common on the eastern cliffs; colour variety yellow.
☐ *Sisymbrium officinale* (Hedge Mustard). First noted 1883 and occasional near Split Rock Battery.
☐ *Arabidopsis thaliana* (Common Wall Cress). First noted 1883 and found again in 1977.

Resedaceae (Mignonette family)

☐ *Reseda luteola* (Weld). First noted in 1923 and common on the South Landing path and at Summit Battery; occasional elsewhere.

Violaceae (Violet family)

☐ *Viola riviniana* (Common Violet). First noted 1909 but no recent record.
☐ *Viola reichenbachiana* (Pale Wood Violet). First noted 1883 but no recent record.

Polygalaceae (Milkwort family)

☐ *Polygala vulgaris* (Common Milkwort). First noted 1891 but no recent record.

Hypericaceae (St John's Wort family)

☐ *Hypericum pulchrum* (Slender St John's Wort). First noted 1883 but no recent record.
☐ *Hypericum montanum* (Mountain St John's Wort). First noted 1890 but no recent record.

Chenopodiaceae (Goosefoot family)

☐ *Chenopodium album* (Fat Hen). First noted 1883 and common around the paths and at the top of the northern cliffs.
☐ *Chenopodium rubrum* (Red Goosefoot). First noted 1883 and occasional particularly on the northern cliffs.
☐ *Beta vulgaris* spp. *maritima* (Sea Beet). First noted 1891 and common on the cliffs.

☐ *Atriplex hastata* (Hastate Orache). First noted in 1883 and present all across the southern cliffs.

☐ *Atriplex patula* (Common Orache). First noted 1883 and recorded again in 1978 and 1988.

☐ *Suaeda maritima* (Herbaceous Seablite). First noted 1881 but no recent record.

☐ *Suaeda fruticosa* (Shrubby Seablite). First noted 1581 but the attribution is doubtful.

☐ *Salsola kali* (Saltwort). First noted 1831 but no recent record.

Caryophyllaceae (Pink family)

☐ *Silene dioica* (Red Campion). First noted 1883, when it was occasional on the northern cliffs, but no record since 1975.

White Campion:
frequent on the northern cliffs, drawn here by Moira Williams and courtesy the Royal Society for Nature Conservation.

☐ *Silene alba* (White Campion). First noted 1891 and occasional at Split Rock and on the northern cliffs.

☐ *Silene alba* x *S. dioica* (Pink Campion). Hybrid, first noted 1977 and occasional at Laboratory Battery.

☐ *Silene vulgaris* (Bladder Campion). First noted 1891 but no recent record.

☐ *Silene maritima* (Sea Campion). First noted 1883 and common on the eastern and northern cliffs.
☐ *Cerastium holosteoides* Common Mouse-ear). First noted 1883 and occasional on the northern cliffs.
☐ *Cerastium glomeratum* (Sticky Mouse-ear). First noted 1883 and found again in 1978.
☐ *Cerastium diffusum* (Dark-green Mouse-ear). First noted 1883 and again in 1977.
☐ *Cerastium pumilum* (Curtis's Mouse-ear). First noted 1891 but no recent record.
☐ *Cerastium semidecandrum* (Little Mouse-ear). First noted 1891 but no recent record.
☐ *Stellaria nemorum* (Wood Chickweed). First noted 1883 but no recent record.
☐ *Stellaria media* (Common Chickweed). First noted 1883 and occasional near the Inn.
☐ *Stellaria neglecta* (Greater Chickweed). First noted 1964 but no recent record.
☐ *Stellaria pallida* (Lesser Chickweed). First noted 1938 and again in 1988.
☐ *Sagina apetala* (Common Pearlwort). First noted 1883 but no recent record.
☐ *Sagina maritima* (Sea Pearlwort). First noted 1952 and occasional on the northern cliffs and Rudder Rock.
☐ *Sagina procumbens* (Procumbent Pearlwort). First noted 1883 and occasional on the northern cliffs.
☐ *Arenaria leptoclados* (Lesser Thyme-leaved Sandwort). First noted 1977 but no recent record.
☐ *Arenaria serpyllifolia* (Thyme-leaved Sandwort). First noted 1836 but no recent record.
☐ *Spergula arvensis* (Corn Spurrey). First noted 1883 but no recent record.
☐ *Spergularia marina* (Lesser Sea Spurrey). First noted 1977 and occasional in the splash-zone of the lower cliffs.

Malvaceae (Mallow family)

☐ *Malva sylvestris* (Common Mallow). First noted 1883 and occasional.
☐ *Malva moschata* (Musk Mallow). First noted 1979, beside the main path to the west of Garden Battery where it survived for a number of years.

☐ *Lavatera arborea* (Tree Mallow). First noted 1773 and common along the southern cliffs, forming what in some years has been a dense canopy of person-sized plants covering the area between the splash-zone and the normal scrub-belt. That was the case in 1978 when I enthused over it in the first book about the island: "This is a true maritime species, withstanding gull guano and gales to bring a defiant splash of purple flowers to the inaccessible top of Rudder Rock, at the extreme tip of the island. A forest of Tree Mallow smothers the undercliff east of Split Rock in an acre belt. Even this scrubby plant, like all the commoner Steep Holm species, had a medicinal role and was used for ointment and poultices. Tree Mallow leaves steeped in hot water soothe sprains. The flowers can be used for dyeing." Its coverage receded to solitary gnarled specimens on exposed crags but a new generation then sprang up across wide areas, including the path up from the Quay, in the mild winter of 1988-89.

Tree Mallow: the largest of the island's maritime species has fleshy dark-green leaves and purple flowers. The picture opposite shows a typical older specimen, firmly rooted on an exposed outcrop. This tree-like biennial can achieve three metres in height.

FLORA, page 67

Linaceae (Flax family)

☐ *Linum catharticum* (Purging Flax). First noted 1891 but no recent record.

Geraniaceae (Geranium family)

☐ *Geranium dissectum* (Cut-leaved Cranesbill). First noted 1883 but no recent record.
☐ *Geranium molle* (Dovesfoot Cranesbill). First noted 1891 and occasional on the northern cliffs.
☐ *Geranium robertianum* (Herb Robert). First noted 1883 and common on the eastern and northern cliffs.
☐ *Geranium robertianum* ssp. *maritimum* (Maritime Herb Robert). First noted 1923 and common on the lower cliffs.
☐ *Erodium maritimum* (Sea Storksbill). First noted 1773 and occasional on the northern cliffs.
☐ *Erodium circutarium* (Common Storksbill). First noted 1883 and probably still occasional on the northern cliffs though there has been no record since the 1970s.

Oxalidaceae (Wood-sorrel family)

☐ *Oxalis acetosella* (Wood-sorrel). First noted 1883 but no recent record.

Aceraceae (Maple family)

☐ *Acer pseudoplatanus* (Sycamore). First noted 1883 and common on the eastern cliffs, where it forms a full wood from the cliff-edge north-east of Cliff Cottage to the Priory on top of the island. The trees were decimated by the 1975-76 droughts but their root systems survived and thrust out new branches. Some of the sycamores that lost their leaves in the second drought year had their biological clocks sent haywire and burst their buds at the end of November, being covered in spring leaves on 5 December 1976. There is much prejudice against Sycamores and on a visit to the island by the Countryside Commission staff I took the opportunity to refer to them as "beautiful trees". Sir Derek Barber, the Commission's chairman, was delighted. "You can repeat that,"he said, "When you have an audience gathered round after lunch."

Papilionaceae (Pea family)

☐ *Genista anglica* (Petty Whin). Noted 1883 but a doubtful record.
☐ *Onosis repens* (Restharrow). First noted 1883 but no recent record.

☐ *Medicago lupulina* (Black Medick). First noted 1891 and again in 1988.
☐ *Trifolium dubium* (Lesser Yellow Trefoil). First noted 1891 but no recent record.
☐ *Trifolium campestre* (Hop Trefoil). First noted 1891 but no recent record.
☐ *Trifolium repens* (White Clover). First noted 1883 and occasional on the northern cliffs.
☐ *Trifolium pratense* (Red Clover). First noted 1891 and reappeared in the Farmhouse ruin in 1979, apparently from seed exposed by clearance work.
☐ *Anthyllis vulneraria* (Kidney Vetch). First noted 1891 but no recent record.
☐ *Lotus corniculatus* (Birdsfoot-trefoil). First noted 1877 and reappeared in plots on the plateau in 1988, probably reintroduced with grass seed.
☐ *Lotus uliginosus* (Large Birdsfoot-trefoil). First noted 1877 but no recent record.
☐ *Vicia hirsuta* (Hairy Tare). First noted 1883 but no recent record.
☐ *Vicia tetrasperma* (Smooth Tare). First noted 1883 but no recent record.
☐ *Vicia sepium* (Bush Vetch). First noted 1909 but no recent record.
☐ *Vicia sativa* (Common Vetch). First noted 1883 but no recent record.
☐ *Vicia sativa* ssp. *angustifolia* (Narrow-leaved Vetch). First noted 1909 but no recent record.
☐ *Vicia lathyroides* (Spring Vetch). First noted 1909 but no recent record.
☐ *Lathyrus pratensis* (Meadow Vetch). First noted 1883 but no recent record.

Rosaceae (Rose family)

☐ *Rubus caesius* (Dewberry). First noted 1964 and occasional in the eastern scrub.
☐ *Rubus ulmifolius* (Bramble species). First noted 1891 and widespread across the top of the island from Summit Battery to the eastern cliff path, and on the southern side from Split Rock to Garden Battery. There is a multiplicity of blackberry sub-species and the island's bushes certainly seem to be varied. Jim Hunt, of Banwell, wrote to me about one of the plants at Garden Battery in 1975: "I

found a high bramble bush by the path, yielding a number of ripe specimens ... noticeably different in being "double blackberries', that is, as if two blackberries had formed side by side — though one was somewhat smaller that its companion. I was too intent on securing ripe fruit to study this phenomenon except to observe that only one such seemed to sport these double blackberries. It may be that such sports are not unknown among brambles elsewhere but it always stuck in my mind that here might be another deviation developing on the island."

☐ *Potentilla reptans* (Creeping Cinquefoil). First noted 1954 and occasional, including 1988.

☐ *Rosa ?canina,* possibly *Rosa micrantha* (Dog Rose group). First noted 1890 and occasional on the eastern cliffs. The species identification is still in doubt.

☐ *Rosa dumalis* (Dog Rose species). First noted 1890 but no recent record.

☐ *Rosa rubiginosa* (Sweet Briar). First noted 1923 but no recent record.

☐ *Prunus spinosa* (Blackthorn). First noted 1938 and occasional, the main clumps being on the north side of Tombstone Battery.

☐ *Crataegus monogyna* (Hawthorn). First noted 1891 and occasional, particularly to the north and the east of the Barracks, where there is a single large tree.

☐ *Sorbus aucuparia* (Rowan). Introduced in 1976 with one specimen surviving, and fruiting, close to Tombstone Battery.

☐ *Sorbus aria* (Whitebeam). Introduced 1980 and occasional with specimens surviving between Rudder Rock Battery and the Barracks. Whitebeam is native to the Mendip Hills and grows from rock faces, as at Burrington Combe. On the island they have proved to be the most successful introduced tree since the Sycamores, and are equally salt resistant.

Crassulaceae (Stonecrop family)

☐ *Sedum telephium* (Orpine). First noted 1883 but no recent record.

☐ *Sedum album* (White Stonecrop). First noted 1981 and still growing on the thin soil at the same concrete Nissen-hut base.

☐ *Sedum acre* (Biting Stonecrop). First noted 1877 and common on the cliffs and ruined walls.

☐ *Umbilicus rupestris* (Wall Pennywort). First noted 1883 and common, particularly in partially-shaded rock crevices in the northern and eastern cliffs.

OPPOSITE — Biting Stonecrop: wall at the Farm, smothered with clusters of yellow stars.

FLORA, page 71

Saxifragaceae (Saxifrage family)

☐ *Saxifraga tridactylites* (Rue-leaved Saxifrage). First noted 1909 and common on the ruined walls of the Tenement but only occasional on other ruins and the northern cliffs.

Grossulariaceae (Currant family)

☐ *Ribes uva-crispa* (Gooseberry). First noted 1923 with one large bush, probably the same one, on the undercliff at the north side of Tower Rock.

Onagraceae (Willowherb family)

☐ *Epilobium montanum* Broad-leafed Willow-herb). First noted 1976 and occasional on the northern top of the island.

Araliaceae (Ivy family)

☐ *Hedera helix* (Ivy). First noted 1831 and common, particularly on the eastern cliffs.

Umbelliferae (Carrot family)

☐ *Sanicula europaea* (Sanicle). First noted 1883 but no recent record.

☐ *Anthriscus sylvestris* (Cow Parsley). First noted 1923 and formerly occasional on the top of the island but no record since the 1970s.

☐ *Torilis japonica* (Upright Hedge-parsley). First noted 1883 but no recent record.

☐ *Coriandrum sativum* (Coriander). First noted before 1791 but no recent record.

☐ *Smyrnium olusatrum* (Alexanders). First noted before 1562 and ubiquitous across the entire island, from the splash-zone and up the cliffs to a "meadow" smothering the top. Grows also beneath the Sycamores and amongst scrub. Tony Parsons estimated in August 1977 that approximately 6,000 seeds are produced, on average, per plant: "This seems a large quantity, but one plant held over 9,000 seeds." From estimating the varying density of the plants in the different types of habitat he calculated there were about 75,000 growing on the island: "This meant that the number of Alexanders seeds produced in one year is roughly 450 million. A large batch of seed was weighed to obtain an average weight, and this indicated that the overall weight of one year's seeds is in the region of 22 tonnes." Soil disturbance, at the Inn and gun batteries, has revealed seeds from historic levels, some of which still proved to be viable. Introduced as a pot-herb, probably by the mediaeval monks.

OPPOSITE — Alexanders: botanists call this a 'meadow' but others use the word 'jungle'. Stinging nettles grow beneath.

FLORA, page 73

Hemlock: classical poison plant, white-lace flowers, parsley-shaped foliage and tall greyish-green stem with purple blotches — beware of dwarf forms that are parsley-like.

☐ *Conium maculatum* (Hemlock). First noted 1773 and common, particularly among the Alexanders and bramble on the northern top of the island. Probably a monastic introduction though it is such a strong poison that its only medical application would be euthanasia. Sometimes the plants are exceedingly high; the tallest found by Tony Parsons in 1978 was 249 cm.

☐ *Petroselinum crispum* (Parsley). First noted 1891 but no recent record.

☐ *Pimpinella saxifraga* (Burnet Saxifrage). First noted 1891 but no recent record.

☐ *Crithmum maritimum* (Rock Samphire). First noted 1773, plentiful in 1831, and still common at Split Rock.
☐ *Aethusa cynapium* (Fool's Parsley). First noted 1877 but no recent record.
☐ *Foeniculum vulgare* (Fennel). First noted 1883 but no recent record.
☐ *Pastinaca sativa* (Wild Parsnip). First noted 1891 but no recent record.
☐ *Heracleum sphondylium* (Hogweed). First noted 1890 but no recent record.

Euphorbiaceae (Spurge family)

☐ *Mercurialis perennis* (Dog's Mercury). First noted 1883 and locally plentiful at the top of the northern cliffs with large areas above 208 Steps and beside the cross-path to the Barracks.
☐ *Mercurialis annua* (Annual Mercury). First noted 1952 and common as a secondary growth beneath the stands of Alexanders on the top of the island.
☐ *Euphorbia lathyrus* (Caper Spurge). First noted 1773 and occasional, particularly to the south-west of the Barracks. Probably a monastic introduction.

Caper Spurge: unmistakeable architectural shape, glossy succulent leaves, and capers, characterise this magnificent milk-plant.

Polygonaceae (Dock family)

☐ *Polygonum aviculare* (Knotgrass main species). First noted 1883 but probably the closely related *P. arenastrum*.

☐ *Polygonum arenastrum* (Knotgrass variant). First noted 1978 and occasional around the Priory and Garden Battery.

☐ *Polygonum persicaria* (Red Shank). First noted 1953 but no recent record.

☐ *Rumex acetosella* (Sheep's Sorrel). First noted 1883 but no recent record.

☐ *Rumex acetosa* (Common Sorrel). First noted 1883 and formerly occasional on the northern cliffs, but no record since 1976.

☐ *Rumex crispus* (Curled Dock). First noted 1891 and occasional in the upper parts of the northern cliffs.

☐ *Rumex obtusifolius* (Broad-leaved Dock). First noted 1975 and occasional on the north side of the island.

Urticaceae (Nettle family)

☐ *Parietaria diffusa* Pellitory-of-the-Wall). First noted 1831 and common on the cliffs and ruined walls.

☐ *Urtica urens* (Small nettle). First noted 1883 and common on the cliffs and amongst scrub.

☐ *Urtica dioica* (Stinging Nettle). First noted 1891 and universal across the top of the island, growing amongst Alexanders and through the bramble and privet scrub.

Fagaceae (Trees)

☐ *Quercus ilex* (Evergreen Oak). Introduced 1974 with one surviving in the ruin of the Tenement, built in 1776, at the eastern end of the island.

☐ *Quercus robur* (Pedunculate Oak). Introduced in the early 1980s with a few survivors west of the Barracks.

Ericaceae (Heathers)

☐ *Arbutus unedo* (Strawberry Tree). Introduced 1975 with a single survivor, deer-browsed, recovering beside the Priory ruin.

Moraceae (Fig Tree)

☐ *Ficus carica* (Fig Tree). First noted 1964 and the same specimen surviving, wind-blown in a crevice on an outcrop half-way down the cliffs, between the Barracks and South Landing. Another grows out

Fig Tree: rising from a cleft in the southern cliffs.

of the wall below the South Landing searchlight post. Others were planted at the east end of the island in 1978.

Plumbaginaceae (Sea-lavender family)

☐ *Limonium vulgare* (Common Sea-lavender). First noted 1773 but probably a misidentification of the Rock Sea-lavender.

☐ *Limonium binervosum* (Rock Sea-lavender). First noted 1883 and common west of South Landing, to Split Rock, though generally only occasional elsewhere on the southern and eastern cliffs. This is an exceedingly variable plant, liable to develop into sub species, and Martin Ingrouille of Leicester University has described Steep Holm specimens as "some of the largest I have ever seen".

☐ *Armeria maritima* (Thrift). First noted 1883 and occasional from Split Rock around Rudder Rock to Summit Battery. Above the latter, inland from the cliff, five flourishing specimens established themselves in the cutting beside the 1941-built eastern fortifications. There are also occasional clumps on the south-west side of Tower Rock.

Primulaceae (Primrose family)

☐ *Primula veris* (Cowslip). First noted 1883, and common in 1907, but no recent record. It was last recorded in 1964.

☐ *Primula vulgaris* (Primrose). First noted 1883 and isolated specimens surviving in the Sycamore wood in the 1970s but current status doubtful.

☐ *Anagallis arvensis* (Scarlet Pimpernel). First noted 1909 and common in cliff-crevices and occasional beside paths.

☐ *Anagallis foemina* (Blue Pimpernel). First noted 1883 but no recent record.

Oleaceae (Trees)

☐ *Fraxinus excelsior* (Ash). Introduced in the 1980s with a few surviving specimens in the eastern scrub.

Buddlejaceae (Buddleja family)

☐ *Buddleja davidii* (Butterfly-bush). Introduced 1974 and occasional in the eastern half of the island.

Oleaceae (Olive family)

☐ *Syringa vulgaris* (Lilac). First noted 1909 but no recent record.
☐ *Ligustrum vulgare* (Wild Privet). First noted 1625 and still common, being the most extensive of the island's scrub species and covering 10 acres; which is 20 percent of the island.

Gentianaceae (Gentian family)

☐ *Centaurium erythraea* (Common Centuary). First noted 1909 but no recent record.

☐ *Blackstonia perfoliata* (Yellow-wort). First noted 1877 but no recent record.

Boraginaceae (Borage family)

☐ *Cynoglossum officinale* (Hound's-tongue). First noted 1877 and occasional beside paths.

☐ *Lycopsis arvensis* (Bugloss). First noted in 1909 and occasional on the northern cliffs and at Split Rock Battery.

☐ *Myosotis scorpioides* (Water Forget-me-not). First noted 1909 but no recent record; there is very little suitable habitat.

☐ *Myosotis arvensis* (Common Forget-me-not). First noted 1891 and occasional throughout the island, being locally common on some parts of the northern cliff.

☐ *Myosotis discolor* (Changing Forget-me-not). First noted 1891 and locally frequent, particularly around Summit Battery and at the Priory.

☐ *Myosotis ramosissima* (Early Forget-me-not). First noted 1891 but no recent record.
☐ *Echium vulgare* (Viper's Bugloss). First noted 1909 but no recent record.

Solanaceae (Nightshade family)

☐ *Atropa belladonna* (Deadly Nightshade). First noted 1977 and represented by a single plant beside the Barracks.

Henbane: downy greyish-green leaves and yellow and purple flowers of a plant that is rare nationally and a probable monastic introduction to Steep Holm, being used in mediaeval, and indeed modern, herbal medicine.

☐ *Hyoscyamus niger* (Henbane). First noted 1831 and occasional across most of the island, being locally common along the cliffs from Split Rock to South Landing. A probable monastic introduction.

FLORA, page 79

☐ *Solanum dulcamara* (Woody Nightshade). First noted 1965 and occasional at Tombstone Battery and across the top of the island.
☐ *Solanum nigrum* (Black Nightshade). First noted 1965 and occasional, particularly on the northern side of the island.
☐ *Solanum tuberosum* (Potato). First noted 1963, and occasionally since, having grown from discarded tubers that have survived mild winters — though the plants found in 1963 could only have been from that season, given the severity of the winter of 1962-63.

Scrophulariaceae (Figwort family)

☐ *Verbascum thapsus* (Great Mullein). First noted 1877 and occasional over most of the island, being locally common on parts of the southern cliff.
☐ *Antirrhinum majus* (Snapdragon). First noted 1891 but no recent record.
☐ *Scrophularia nodosa* (Common Figwort). First noted 1891 and common over much of the eastern end of the island. Clearance of soil from the Inn has spread the seed further and it is now plentiful beside the lower section of the eastern cliff.
☐ *Digitalis purpurea* (Foxglove). First noted 1891 but no recent record.
☐ *Veronica chamaedrys* (Germander Speedwell). First noted 1891 but no recent record.
☐ *Veronica serpyllifolia* (Thyme-leafed Speedwell). First noted 1883 but no recent record.
☐ *Veronica arvensis* (Wall Speedwell). First noted 1891 and present in 1977 and 1987.
☐ *Veronica persica* (Buxbaum's Speedwort). First noted 1891 and occasional on the northern cliffs.
☐ *Veronica agrestis* (Field Speedwort). First noted 1923 but no recent record.
☐ *Veronica polita* (Grey Field Speedwell) First noted 1988, by Liz McDonnell.
☐ *Euphrasia officinalis* aggregate (Eyebright group of species). First noted 1883 but no recent record.
☐ *Odontites verna* (Red Bartsis). First noted 1883 but no recent record.

Orobanchaceae (Broomrape family)

☐ *Orobanche hederae* (Ivy Broomrape). First noted 1946 and occasional amongst the dense growths of ivy on the eastern cliffs.

Ivy Broomrape: flowering shoots of this root-parasite, which attaches its underground tubers to the roots of the Ivy (leaves of which are glimpsed top left and bottom right) photographed beside the main path on the east cliff by Maurice Hanssen on 13 August 1977.

Verbenaceae (Verbena family)

☐ *Verbena officinalis* (Vervain). First noted 1883 but no recent record.

Labiatae (Mint family)

☐ *Thymus drucei* (Thyme). First noted 1883 but no recent record.

☐ *Calamintha ascendens* (Common Calamint). First noted 1891 and occasional between the Inn and Cliff Cottage and on the southern slopes.

☐ *Prunella vulgaris* (Self-heal). First noted 1938 but no recent record.

☐ *Ballota nigra* (Black Horehound). First noted 1883 but no recent record.

☐ *Lamium amplexicaule* (Henbit). First noted 1890 and occasional on the northern cliffs.

☐ *Lamium maculatum* (Spotted Dead-nettle). First noted 1883 but no recent record.

☐ *Lamium hybridum* (Cut-leaved Dead Nettle). First noted 1978 and occasional near Laboratory Battery.

☐ *Lamium purpureum* (Red Dead-nettle). First noted 1975 and locally common on the top of the island.

☐ *Glechoma hederacea* (Ground Ivy). First noted 1883 and carpets the top of the island being the ground-cover plant beneath the meadow of Alexanders.

☐ *Marrubium vulgare* (White Horehound). First noted 1883 but no recent record.

☐ *Teucrium chamaedyrs* (Wall Germander). First noted 1877 but no recent record.

☐ *Teucrium scorodonia* (Woodsage). First noted 1831 and widespread, being locally common in parts of the Alexanders meadow.

Plantaginaceae (Plantain family)

☐ *Plantago major* (Greater Plantain). First noted 1953 and occasional on the northern cliffs.

☐ *Plantago media* (Hoary Plantain). First noted 1883 but no recent record.

☐ *Plantago lanceolata* (Ribwort Plantain). First noted 1883 and occasional on the northern cliffs.

☐ *Plantago maritima* (Sea Plantain). First noted 1883 but no recent record.

☐ *Plantago coronopus* var *sabrinae* (Buckshorn Plantain). First noted from before 1845 and in the past claimed as a separate species though

Buckshorn Plantain: Steep Holm speciality, the variant or ecad unique to the island, in a particularly lush specimen on an outcrop above the sea at Split Rock, showing its characteristic succulent serrated leaves and distinctive spikes of flower, photographed by Steven Murdoch on 20 April 1989 (a day that will live in infamy: the centenary of Hitler's birth).

it is now regarded as an ecad of *Plantago coronopus* that is "a very striking variation of this variable species". It is generally occasional on the cliffs, in crevices and ledges, and locally common on the lower outcrops of Rudder Rock, Split Rock, South Landing and around Tower Rock. The plants were particularly large and spreading, frequently making lush clumps, in the mild 1988-89 winter.

Campanulaceae (Bellflower family)

☐ *Campanula latifolia* (Giant Bellflower). First noted 1883 but no recent record.
☐ *Campanula rotundifolia* (Harebell). First noted 1883 but no recent record.

Rubiaceae (Bedstraw family)

☐ *Sherardia arvensis* (Field Madder). First noted 1891 and occurred annually on the Priory site in the late 1980s, probably from seed disturbed by excavation.
☐ *Galium cruciata* (Crosswort). First noted 1883 but no recent record.
☐ *Galium mollugo* (Hedge Bedstraw). First noted 1890 but no recent record.
☐ *Galium verum* (Lady's Bedstraw). First noted 1883 and occasional on the east side of Summit Battery.
☐ *Galium saxatile* (Heath Bedstraw). First noted 1938 but no recent record.
☐ *Galium aparine* (Cleavers). First noted 1883 and occasional on the northern cliffs.
☐ *Rubia peregrina* (Wild Madder). First noted 1891 but no recent record.

Caprifoliaceae (Honeysuckle family)

☐ *Sambucus nigra* (Elder). First noted circa 1625, and by 1831 said to be reduced to a single tree close to the Monks' Well, but now widespread across the entire island apart from the most exposed and soilless areas of cliff.
☐ *Symphoricarpos rivularis* (Snowberry). First noted 1909 but no recent record.

Valerianaeae (Valerian family)

☐ *Centranthus ruber* (Red Valerian). First noted 1883 and locally common on the eastern cliffs around the Inn and Cliff Cottage, from where it was probably a nineteenth century garden escape.

Dipsacaceae (Teasel family)

☐ *Dispacus fullonum* (Teasel). First noted 1891 and common on the eastern top of the island.

Compositae (Daisy family)

☐ *Helianthus annuus* (Sunflower). First noted 1965 and occasional on the northern top of the island.

☐ *Senecio jacobaea* (Ragwort). First noted 1831 and locally common, with many extensive patches on the top of the island, and occasional on both the north and south cliffs.
☐ *Senecio squalidus* (Oxford Ragwort). First noted 1962 but no recent record.
☐ *Senecio viscosus* (Stinking Grounsel). First noted 1883 but no recent record.
☐ *Senecio vulgaris* (Grounsel). First noted 1883 and common beside paths and on the northern cliffs.
☐ *Senecio vulgaris* var. *radiatus* (Grounsel, rayed form). First noted 1953 and occasional on the northern cliffs.
☐ *Tussilago farfara* (Coltsfoot). First noted 1883 but no recent record.
☐ *Inula conyza* (Ploughman's Spikenard). First noted 1883 but no recent record.
☐ *Inula crithmoides* (Golden Samphire). First noted 1773 and "plentiful" in 1831, which is still the case, with a number of fine specimens on the southern cliffs, particularly around South Landing and Reservoir Cavity.
☐ *Filago germanica* (Cudweed). First noted in 1883 but no recent record.
☐ *Filagi minima* (Slender Cudweed). First noted 1887 but no recent record.
☐ *Bellis perennis* (Daisy). First noted 1883 and occasional in the grass that fringes the top of the northern cliffs, and also at the approach to South Landing.
☐ *Tripleurospermum maritimum* (Scentless Mayweed). First noted 1979 and occasional on the top of the island and the north-west cliffs.
☐ *Chrysanthemum segetum* (Corn Marigold). First noted 1883 but no recent record.
☐ *Chrysanthemum vulgare* (Ox-eye Daisy). First noted 1883 and common on the eastern cliffs.
☐ *Sonchus asper* (Prickly Sow-thistle). First noted 1963 and occasional.
☐ *Sonchus oleraceus* (Smooth Sow-thistle). First noted 1891 but no recent record.
☐ *Hieracium murorum, sensu lato* − i.e. loosely; in a wide sense (Common Hawkweed). First noted 1883 but no recent record.
☐ *Hieracum pilosella* (Mouse-ear Hawkweed). First noted 1891 but no recent record.
☐ *Crepis capillaris* (Smooth Hawksbeard). First noted 1891 and occasional.
☐ *Taraxacum officinale* (Dandelion). First noted 1890 and common on

the cliffs and beside paths.

☐ *Taraxacum laevigatum* (Lesser Dandelion). First noted 1890 and occasional on the northern and eastern cliffs.

☐ *Carlina vulgaris* (Carline Thistle). First noted 1883 but no recent record.

☐ *Arctium lappa* (Greater Burdock). First noted 1887 but no recent record.

☐ *Arctium pubens* (Lesser Burdock). First noted 1909 and common beside paths in the eastern half of the island.

☐ *Carduus tenuiflorus* (Slender Thistle). First noted 1952 and common on the southern cliffs, particularly at Split Rock.

☐ *Carduus nutans* (Musk Thistle). First noted 1877 but no recent record.

☐ *Carduus acanthoides* (Welted Thistle). First noted 1883 but no recent record.

☐ *Cirsium vulgare* (Spear Thistle). First noted 1966 and occasional on the southern cliffs.

☐ *Cirsium arvense* (Creeping Thistle). First noted 1883 and occasional on the northern cliffs.

☐ *Cirsium acaulon* (Stemless Thistle). First noted 1883 but no recent record.

☐ *Silybum marianum* (Mediterranean Milk Thistle). First noted 1967 and again in 1977 with a single splendid specimen growing beside the path to the east of the Barracks, but no recent record. The 1977 plant was a casual arrival, its seed wind-blown from the Mediterranean in the hot summer of 1976, and several plants arrived from the same source on Brean Down and in many other parts of southern England.

☐ *Centaurea scabiosa* (Greater Knapweed). First noted 1883 but no recent record.

☐ *Centaurea nigra* (Lesser Knapweed). First noted 1883 but no recent record.

☐ *Lapsana communis* (Nipplewort). First noted 1883 and occasional on the northern cliffs.

☐ *Hypochaeris radicata* (Common Cat's Ear). First noted 1883 and formerly occasional on the cliffs, but no record since 1976.

☐ *Leontodon autumnalis* (Autumn Hawkbit). First noted 1891 but no recent record.

☐ *Leontodon hispidus* (Rough Hawkbit). First noted 1891 but no recent record.

☐ *Picris echioides* (Bristly Ox-tongue). First noted 1891 but no recent record.

Amaryllidaceae (Bulbous herb family)

☐ *Galanthus nivalis* (Snowdrop). First noted on 1 April 1978, when it was setting seed. Occasional with small clumps apparently surviving in the Sycamore wood though they are in an area subject to landslips.

Liliaceae (Lily family)

☐ *Endymion non-scriptus* (Bluebell). First noted 1883 and occasional, with a clump surviving between the Barracks and Farmhouse, though plants that were still present in the Sycamore wood in the 1970s seem to have been lost in landslips.

Wild Leek: cliffside clump — they produce bulbous flower heads but do not yield fertile seed, clusters like this being achieved by the outward spread of bulblets.

☐ *Allium ampeloprasum* (Wild Leek). First noted from before 1625 and common on the eastern cliffs. Probable monastic introduction. This is a cytologically diverse species and the specimens on Steep

Holm represent its mediaeval cultivated stock; of which, in the Sloane Herbarium, the island has provided the lectotype. The bulbs have the chromosomes 2n=48 and are the Wild Leek senso stricto, as designated for its Latin specific name by Linnaeus, not that he ever saw the plant.

Iridaceae (Iris family)

☐ *Iris foetidissima* (Stinking Iris). First noted 1877 and common across the top of the island and on the southern cliffs; occasional on the northern cliffs.

Orchidaceae (Orchid family)

☐ *Ophrys apifera* (Bee Orchid). First noted 1887 but no recent record.

☐ *Orchis mascula* (Early Purple Orchid). First noted 1883 but no recent record.

Araceae (Arum family)

☐ *Arum maculatum* (Cuckoo Pint). First noted 1831 and common on the eastern cliffs; occasional on the southern side of the island.

OPPOSITE — Wild Leek: flower-heads projecting from the eastern cliff.

Cyperaceae (Sedge family)

☐ *Carex flacca* (Carnation Grass). First noted 1907 but no recent record.

Gramineae (Grass family)

☐ *Bromus sterilis* (Barren Brome). First noted 1891 but no recent record.
☐ *Bromus erectus* (Upright Brome). First noted 1883 and occasional on the northern cliffs.
☐ *Bromus hordeaceus* (Soft Brome). First noted 1883 but no recent record.
☐ *Hordeum murinum* (Wall Barley). First noted 1883 and occasional on the southern cliffs.
☐ *Hordeum secalinum* (Meadow Barley). First noted 1883 but no recent record.
☐ *Hordeum distichon* (Barley cultivar). First noted 1979 on the eastern cliffs.
☐ *Festuca ovina* (Sheep's Fescue). First noted 1891 and locally common along the top edge of the northern cliffs and in the remnants of the former gull-lawns on the top of the island.
☐ *Festuca longifolia* (Hard Fescue). First noted 1883 but no recent record.
☐ *Festuca rubra* (Creeping Fescue). First noted 1883 and common in a number of places.
☐ *Festuca nigrescens* (Chewing's Fescue). First noted 1923 but no recent record.
☐ *Festuca rubra* var. *pruinosa* (Salt-marsh Fescue). First noted 1953 but no recent record.
☐ *Festuca pratensis* (Meadow Fescue). First noted 1883 but no recent record.
☐ *Festuca loliaceum* (Hybrid Fescue). First noted 1923 but no recent record.
☐ *Lolium perenne* (Perennial Rye-grass). First noted 1883 and occasional on the plateau towards the east end of the island.
☐ *Poa trivialis* (Rough Meadow-grass). First noted 1954 and occasional in the former "gull lawn" on the eastern plateau.
☐ *Poa pratensis* (Smooth Meadow-grass). First noted 1883 but no recent record.
☐ *Poa subcaerulea* (Spring Meadow-grass). First noted 1891 and re-

corded by Liz McDonnell in 1988.

☐ *Poa annua* (Annual Poa). First noted 1883 and occasional at many sites on the cliffs and plateau.

☐ *Brachypodium sylvaticum* (Slender False-brome). First noted 1891 and occasional on the eastern plateau.

☐ *Elymus repens* (Lyme Grass). First noted 1988 and occasional in the Priory ruin.

☐ *Desmazeria rigidum* (Fern Grass). First noted in 1877 and recorded in 1977 and 1988.

☐ *Desmazeria marinum* (Stiff Sand-grass). First noted 1923 and common near the tide-line and on the western cliffs.

☐ *Briza media* (Quaking Grass). First noted 1891 but no recent record.

☐ *Dactylis glomerata* (Cocksfoot). First noted 1883 and occasional along the top edge of the northern cliffs.

☐ *Dactylis glomerata* var. *collina* (Cocksfoot variant). First noted 1923 but no recent record.

☐ *Helictotrichon pubescens* (Hairy Oat-grass). First noted 1891 but no recent record.

☐ *Helictotrichon pratense* (Meadow Oat-grass). First noted 1883 but no recent record.

☐ *Arrhenatherum elatius* (False Oat-grass). First noted 1883 and recorded in 1977 and subsequently.

☐ *Trisetum flavescens* (Golden Oat-grass). First noted 1883 but no recent record.

☐ *Aira caryophyllea* (Silvery Hair-grass). First noted 1883 but no recent record.

☐ *Anthoxanthum odoratum* (Sweet Vernal-grass). First noted 1883 but no recent record.

☐ *Phalaris canariensis* (Canary Grass). First noted 1965 and occasional on the southern cliffs.

☐ *Agrostis canina* (Brown Bent-grass). First noted 1883 but no recent record.

☐ *Agrostis stolonifera* (Creeping Bent). First noted 1883 and common on the plateau.

Exotica

☐ *Entata gigas* (Liane). First noted in 1982 when Jenny Smith found a large seed at the east end of the island. Not that the plant had grown there. It occurs 4,000 miles to the south-west, in the Caribbean, and its seeds drift to Europe on the Gulf Stream. The specimen Jenny found measured 51 x 45 x 18 mm and weighed 23 grams.

Lichen ecology

Dr Oliver Gilbert studied the lichens of Steep Holm in 1980 and expanded the species list from 22 – collected in 1923 – to 96. He was surprised to find the lichen ecology resembled that of an urban gravestone being used as a bird perch. Guano had eutrophicated so much of the exposed limestone that crustose lichens, which would otherwise be dominant, were reduced to a rarity. Instead the yellow rosettes of ☐ *Candelariella medians* had spread with such vigour that it had formed what was in all probability its best colony in the British Isles.

On the east-facing cliff above the Inn, Dr Gilbert discovered a citrine-green variant of that species, a chemotype form not previously described and which would be designated ☐ *Candelariella medians* f. *steepholmensis* in 1981.

Elsewhere on the bird cliffs, other of these larger and more loosely gripping lichens predominated, with the association of what Dr Gilbert termed nitrophiles extending to include ☐ *Xanthoria parietina*, ☐ *Lecania erysibe*, ☐ *Phaeophyscia orbicularis*, ☐ *Physcia adscendens*, ☐ *Rinodina gennarii* and ☐ *Verrucaria viridula*.

Apart from its unique form of *Candelariella medians*, the cliff above the Inn was unusual in still having sizable patches of ☐ *Aspicilia calcarea* and similar species less tolerant of nitrate pollution. Others included ☐ *Agonimia tristicula*, ☐ *Caloplaca aurantia*, ☐ *Caloplaca saxicola*, ☐ *Catapyrenium lachneum*, ☐ *Cladonia pocillum*, ☐ *Lecanora crenulata*, ☐ *Placynthium nigrum* and ☐ *Solenopsora candicans*.

This refuge of the island's older lichen flora probably owes its survival to the double factors of climate – the sun goes off it early in the day – and low intensity seabird use due to the disturbance caused by the zig-zag path being coupled with the obstructions of overhanging sycamore trees. In the wood itself, though it only developed during the first half of the twentieth century, the damp and sheltered rock faces are covered with ☐ *Acrocordia conoidea*, ☐ *Caloplaca cirrochroa*, ☐ *Opegrapha conferta* and ☐ *Porina linearis*.

Other island habitats are also specific and recent. ☐ *Candelariella vitellina* has its single niche on the two Victorian cannon at Split Rock Battery and those on the northern cliffs have a profusion of ☐ *Lecanora dispersa*, whilst the entrances to the underground magazines constructed in 1867 provide mini-caves that offer opportunities for ☐ *Bacidia arnoldiana,* which is rare nationally, and a short stretch of retaining wall beside the path has the only island clusters of the lime-loving ☐ *Protoblastenia rupestris* and ☐ *Toninia aromatica* which are normally common in limestone country.

Other specific localised conditions include the Welsh sandstone ashlars of the Barracks and their occasional insets of white granite. These offer an acidic micro-terrain and on the south, sea-facing, side they support ☐ *Ramalina fastigiata* and ☐ *Ramalina subfarinacea,* whilst on the sheltered northern side there are patches of ☐ *Psilolechia lucida* which is a positively non-lime species.

Where nature provides its own acidic microhabitats is on the crystal and mineral veins that thread the northern cliffs. Here Dr Gilbert found several maritime species and described their zonation upwards from the tide-line. The lowest lichens are in a littoral band which stains the rocks black up to the high-tide mark and into the splashed area above. These species are ☐ *Arthopyrenia halodytes,* ☐ *Verrucaria ditmarsica* and ☐ *Verrucaria mucosa.*

☐ *Verrucaria maura* links these with the next belt, where ☐ *Caloplaca marina* and ☐ *Lecanora helicopis* are the last of the exclusively maritime species, apart from very occasional patches of ☐ *Ramalina siliquosa* which was unusual in being the only grey-coloured lichen mixed in with an otherwise abrupt transition to the orange species of the island as a whole.

OPPOSITE — Wrack-beds: shoreline rock-pools at the north-east corner of the island, part of the fifteen acres of 'underwater' island that emerges twice a day.

MARINE BIOLOGY, page 93

Marine biology

The shore fauna and flora of Steep Holm becomes visible at low-tide. When there are exceptionally high tides, in the region of 13 metres, the water also goes out a long way. There are extensive wrack beds, principally ☐ Saw Wrack and ☐ Bladder Wrack, in the rock-pools below Tower Rock and around the tide-covered Calf Rock. Only in this upper zone is there sufficient light for a reasonable marine fauna as well — but its extent is also limited by the low salinity of the estuarine waters and the high turbidity.

A strong tide-flow causes turbulence off the island's eastern beach and it is only in the relative calm of the south-eastern corner between there and South Landing that marine flora and fauna of any complexity have been able to develop.

Two particular groups of species have problems. Sea-urchins find the water too brackish and the cilia-type creatures which sift food from the water through their waving arms find that there is too much mud in constant suspension for the process to work.

On the other hand there are a number of successful species. Across the sharply pitted bare rocks ☐ Common Limpets, *Patella vulgata*, are everywhere, as are lesser numbers of a second Limpet species, and there are noticeable numbers of a species each of Mail-shell and Whelk and three species of Periwinkles. ☐ The Dog-whelk, *Nucella lapillus*, was particularly abundant when Tony Parsons investigated the eastern side of the shingle spit in October 1986. He found "huge numbers" of "many different colour varieties" along with large numbers of the ☐ Barnacle, *Eliminius modestus*, and many Worm-tubes, believed to be ☐ *Sabellaria alveolata*.

☐ The Beadlet Anemone, *Actinia equina*, is common to the west, in the higher gulleys and cracks where the movement of the water with each tide prevents an accumulation of mud. They are usually maroon to brownish-red but as with the Dog-whelk there can be considerable colour variation and dark-green specimens have been found. Lower down the shore, apparently more tolerant of mud, the ☐ Dahlia Anemone, *Tealia felina*, is reasonably common. Much scarcer, at the other tidal extreme of the splash-zone at the top, is the ☐ Cave Anemone, *Sagartia troglodytes*, which Maurice Yonge found in 1938 in the cleaner spray-pools.

OPPOSITE — Tony Parsons: in usual dress and habitat, with bird-bags (specimens for weighing, ringing and release) hanging from an Elder tree. Most of the information in this book is the result of his work, which began in 1975.

THE NATURALIST, page 95

Subject index

Bats 47
Beetles 57
Birds 4-40
Butterflies 54-55
Cockroaches 57
Crickets 56
Deer 43-46
Dragonflies 55-56
Fleas 57
Flies 56
Flora 58-90
Grasses 89-90
Grasshoppers 56
Hedgehogs 42-43
Invertebraes 51-57
Ladybirds 56
Lichens 91-92

Mammals 41-47
Map 2-3
Marine biology 93-94
Moths 54-55
Muntjac 43-46
Plants 58-94
Porpoises 47
Rabbits 41
Seals 47
Shore fauna and flora 93-94
Slow-worms 48-50
Slugs 52
Snails 51
Spiders 53-54
Woodlice 52

COVER CAPTIONS - the Cormorant is nesting on a ledge of the northern cliffs; a Great Black-backed Gull dives from an outcrop as a Herring Gull watches; Slow-worms copulate on one of the few patches of island turf. Colin Graham photographed the birds and Chris Maslen the reptiles. Wildlife generally is requested to desist from copulating in front of the visitors.

Other books on the island, also by Rodney Legg:

THE STEEP HOLM GUIDE
STEEP HOLM LEGENDS AND HISTORY
STEEP HOLM AT WAR
STEEP HOLM - ALLSOP ISLAND